THESE QUESTIONS CAME FROM PEOPLE JUST
LIKE YOU.
THE ANSWERS
CAN HELP YOU GET
YOUR SHARE OF AN INHERITANCE . . .
INSURE YOUR FAMILY'S FUTURE . . .
AND SAVE YOUR PEACE OF MIND.

QUESTION # 1: My widowed sister was recently killed in a car accident. She had no will, but she once wrote a letter asking me to take care of her kids if anything happened to her. Will I get custody of the children if my mother fights me?

ANSWER: THE LETTER IS NOT LEGALLY BINDING. BUT THERE'S A WAY TO AVOID THIS KIND OF TRAGIC DISPUTE. FIND OUT HOW . . .

QUESTION # 2: I have been living with someone for the past seven years. We have never gone through a legal ceremony or gotten a marriage license, but we consider ourselves married. If he gives me a car, will there be a gift tax?

ANSWER: IT DEPENDS ON THE STATE WHERE THE COUPLE RESIDES. FIND OUT WHICH ONES RECOGNIZE THIS COUPLE AS MARRIED . . .

QUESTION # 3: I own a farm in Nebraska that's been in my family for three generations. I want to leave it to my children, but they all have other careers and know nothing about farming. Is there anything I can do to ensure that it stays in the family for my grandchildren?

ANSWER: SETTING LIMITS ON THE USE OF PROPERTY MADE AS A GIFT AFTER DEATH IS TRICKY. FIND OUT THE FACTS ABOUT "DEAD HAND" CONTROL IN . . .

**THE FIVE-MINUTE LAWYER'S GUIDE TO
ESTATE PLANNING**

Look for these other
FIVE-MINUTE LAWYER'S GUIDES from Dell

THE FIVE-MINUTE LAWYER'S GUIDE TO DIVORCE

THE FIVE-MINUTE LAWYER'S GUIDE TO
BAD DEBTS, CREDIT PROBLEMS, AND
BANKRUPTCY

THE FIVE-MINUTE LAWYER'S GUIDE TO
FEDERAL INCOME TAXES

THE FIVE-MINUTE LAWYER'S

GUIDE TO

ESTATE PLANNING

—

MICHAEL ALLAN CANE

A DELL BOOK

A Note to the Reader:

This book is not intended to be a substitute for the services, legal or otherwise, of a qualified professional. This book will not answer all the questions that the reader may have regarding a particular legal matter. The publisher and author therefore strongly advise that the reader seek professional advice for any such questions or matters.

The author and publisher are not rendering any professional advice, legal or otherwise, in this book. Due to the changing nature of the laws and legal principles discussed in this book, some material may become outdated. If any information is used from this book, it is the reader's responsibility to make sure that the facts and general information are applicable to his or her situation in the relevant state and that there are no applicable changes in the law.

Published by
Dell Publishing
a division of
Bantam Doubleday Dell Publishing Group, Inc.
1540 Broadway
New York, New York 10036

Tele-Lawyer® is a registered trademark of Tele-Lawyer, Inc.

The trademark Dell® is registered in the U.S. Patent and Trademark Office.

ISBN: 0-440-21764-4

Printed in the United States of America

Published simultaneously in Canada

May 1995

10 9 8 7 6 5 4 3 2 1

RAD

To my son,
Joshua Harrison Cane,
who has given me a reason to
do my own estate planning.

About the Series

It was about eighteen years ago when I arrived home following the last of my first-year law school exams. Though too young to have beard stubbles, my red eyes and white, pasty skin told the story of my ordeal. All I could remember of the preceding two weeks was a constant headache and sniffles (which miraculously cleared up just prior to each exam, and returned just following). The legal rules and cases that I had so feverishly crowded into my head were already blurred. It was a horrendous experience in which the only pleasure to be found was in abbreviated sleep and periodic showers (once every three days, whether I needed one or not).

So you will understand that my only thought on that

night was to lapse immediately into a deep coma. Unfortunately, my parents had other plans for the evening.

I entered the house at around seven o'clock to find a small but noisy dinner party going on in the dining room. I'm sure my parents and the guests could see, as I dragged my near-lifeless body through the front door, that I was not in the mood to discuss my adventures in torts; but that didn't seem to subvert the group's good cheer. They waved me to the table, insisting that I be seated and tell them all about "the law school experience." I muttered a few things, such as maybe dentistry wouldn't be as bad as I originally thought, and they all laughed (except my parents, who had helped pay for the year).

I was just about to politely excuse myself when a plate full of meat and vegetables was placed on the table in front of me and a doctor friend of my stepfather's said, "I've got one for you. Tell me what you think about this. . . ." He proceeded to ramble on about a bad investment his ex-accountant (he emphasized the *ex*) had helped him find, and then asked me what he should do.

I was momentarily stunned. He genuinely appeared to be seeking my opinion. Here I was, mere hours after finishing my first year of law school, and this doctor, no less, was seeking my opinion on a legal matter. My exhaustion faded behind a sharp adrenaline rush, and I began to expound at length on liability for breach of contract and fraud.

Over the years I have come to respond to these party-time legal questions with more caution and less enthusiasm. It's not that my ego doesn't still perk up when people come to me seeking advice—it does—it's just that I, like most other attorneys after a dozen or more years in practice, have realized that there is little reward and certain risks in shooting answers from the hip at parties.

What I learned that night is what every second-year law student knows: everyone has a legal question. It took me several more years, however, before I understood why these people would turn to the likes of a first-year law student for their answers. (I had wrongly assumed that word of my great intellectual skills had encouraged the doctor to seek my counsel.)

The reason, I believe, is simply that access to legal information and services is terrible and getting worse. In a recent study, the New York State Bar Association found, to no one's surprise, that low-income people in New York were systematically denied legal services for civil problems. Similar studies in California and other states show this problem to be even more widespread, including most middle-income individuals. The June 3, 1991, issue of the *Wall Street Journal* reported that self-representation in civil law suits is on the rise, citing legal costs and economic pressures as the cause. The American Bar Association Consortium on Legal Services and the Public, in a report published in 1989, stated: "Cost remains a significant element in the decision to seek legal assistance. Those considering consulting lawyers are most likely to refrain from doing so in the case of consumer and marital problems."

Study after study seems to verify that this problem of access to legal services is becoming more and more serious. Part of the problem, as I found out early in my career, is that answering simple questions or handling "small" problems is not a very cost-effective activity for any attorney. Attorneys find party-time questions annoying, because it's not work for which they can bill. Even at the office, answering a client's call for a simple question unattached to a billing item (unless on retainer) often does not make economic sense.

Afraid of liability for client misunderstandings or misapplication, or for giving the wrong off-the-cuff advice, attorneys in such cases will either politely decline to answer the question, usually with some excuse such as "Sorry, but that's not my specialty. You really should see . . ." or offer to research the problem and get back to the client with a confirming memorandum (all of which is charged at a rate that includes time for drafting, analyzing, and researching the question, and takes several weeks).

On the other side, clients are afraid of, and have often experienced, these responses. What they want is a quick answer, not a brush-off or someone making a federal case out of their problem. Consequently, they seek the "party question" route or look to nonprofessional advice—such as Uncle Fred, who three years back had a friend who went through a similar problem. The results are often less than satisfactory.

It was out of this need the Tele-Lawyer was born—a legal advice and information service designed specifically to solve this problem.

Even so, general acceptance of this new type of legal access has not been easy to obtain. Whenever I introduce the Tele-Lawyer concept of legal practice to someone new, I invariably get a raised eyebrow and subtle smirk. "A 900 number, eh?" "Attorneys, yeah, sure." Then when they see that I'm serious, the probing questions start.

From the nonlawyers: But . . . how do you handle

court cases over the phone? What if I need something drawn up or I have to come into the office? Can you write a letter or make a call for me?

From lawyers: But . . . how do you handle the malpractice problem? [This is always the first question from attorneys.] What happens if the client doesn't give you all the information, or lies? What do you charge for research? What do you do with the calls you can't answer over the phone—bring them into the office, refer them out? What would you charge me to be on your referral list?

To these and other similar questions, I politely answer, "You miss the point."

Tele-Lawyer is *not* a traditional law office with a 900 phone number, or a pre-paid legal plan or referral line in disguise. It is something quite different. The company represents a completely new form of access to legal information and services. You pick up the phone and you get an experienced attorney to answer your question. No complications, no frills, no hidden agenda.

A few years back, some friends of mine came up with the concept of using self-help books in combination with independent paralegals to fill the growing gap between the average person and the legal profession. Self-help legal books are easy-to-follow manuals designed to assist individuals in handling their own legal problems: preparing a simple will, filing for a divorce, or even fighting a traffic ticket. Independent paralegals are individuals who are not associated with a particular attorney, but who are experienced and trained in the art of preparing legal forms and making sure they get filed in the proper place.

My friends felt that providing people with accurate

and understandable legal information in the form of self-help books, combined with the experience and support of a trained independent paralegal, would be a viable way of getting people through certain types of legal problems without the expense of hiring an attorney. One limitation of this model for delivery of legal services, as they envisioned it, is that certain questions, because of inexperience, lack of training, or state law, cannot be answered by paralegals, but require a trained, licensed attorney. How to get the answers to these questions without going through the hassle and cost of a law office visit was the real problem.

As luck would have it, the three of us met up, and they adopted Tele-Lawyer as the solution to this problem: the third edge of their triangle.

Tele-Lawyer is simply a source of quick, convenient, cost-effective legal advice from experienced, licensed attorneys. There are no hidden charges, no referrals, no tricks. What you see (or hear) is what you get. A client calls in, gives a brief description of the problem, and is routed to a licensed professional who answers his or her question in, on average, five to ten minutes. Ergo the title "The Five-Minute Lawyer."

Whether the question is critical but simple, like the woman who called after being beaten by her husband and was afraid to leave because he told her if she did she would forfeit her rights to the kids and the house ["Is this true?" she asked. "Of course not!" the attorney answered], or whether it's simple and (seemingly) stupid, like the landlord who wanted to know if he could legally (and literally) toss his tenant and his things out into the street for missing a rent payment [not without the proper notice and court action], we seem to get them all. And now after over five years of operation and tens of thousands of questions (logged and entered into our computer database), we think we have the most complete and accurate idea of the legal questions most often on the minds of Americans today.

We also have the answers.

It is this knowledge that I propose to offer you, the reader, in this Five-Minute Lawyer series. The series is generally a collection of the most frequently asked questions heard by the Tele-Lawyer attorneys over our phone lines, excluding tell-tale information that might breach the confidence of our clients. I also provide a few actual "war stories" of my own to illustrate some of the reasons for our answers.

One piece of advice before you start: every situation is different, sometimes only subtly so, but different nonetheless. This means that even if the facts of a question described in this book—or any of the other books in this series—seem similar to your circumstances, be cautious before applying the answer given. A slight variation can require a different approach, and, of course, you may misapply the law as provided. In addition, the laws of different states may create different results. You will find references to this throughout the book. Take this as a warning against quick, broad applications of the answers provided.

In short, this book and the others in the series are not substitutes for careful, professional analysis of a legal problem or question, they are simply learning tools that may help raise awareness of right or legal issues of which the reader is unaware. They may also provide the right answer. Just be careful when applying the answers provided to different personal situations.

This book is designed for reading by the average person, and thus does not require a legal interpreter or a law degree to understand. It also does not contain a complete discussion of all issues involved in the legal topic area. Quite the contrary, it is designed, as with all books in this series, to be limited to only those questions most commonly asked and therefore of greatest interest to the average person with that type of legal problem.

By buying this book you will also be entitled for a limited time to try out Tele-Lawyer for yourself with up to five minutes of your call free (a $15 value). A phone number and explanation of how to obtain this benefit is contained at the end of this book. I know you will be pleased at this help you receive, and, if not, feel free to call me direct over our toll-free number, 1-800-TELELAW, and I will investigate the problem. You have my word on it.

In addition, if you need a legal document prepared, but do not want to go through the hassle and expense of hiring an attorney to handle the entire case or matter, you may also wish to take advantage of Tele-Lawyer's new LawChoice℗ referral services. Like the regular Tele-Lawyer advice and information program, LawChoice℗ provides you with choices as to how you can approach and handle legal problems affordably.

To use this service you simply call 1-800-TELELAW (635-3520), toll free. A trained operator will examine your needs and offer you a choice of several alternative legal help sources, with their associated costs: self-help books, independent paralegals, mediators, government information sources and attorneys, in addition to legal advice and information over the phone from Tele-Lawyer. An explanation of the advantages and limitations of each of these sources of legal help is available to all callers. Along with ways of combining them to obtain the needed support at the lowest cost.

Call with any questions and inform the operator that you obtained the number from this book to receive information about discounts available for services provided through Tele-Lawyer.

Sometimes entertaining and sometimes sad, the stories we hear, day in and day out, always seem to reinforce our belief that people need to know more about their legal rights and take more control of their legal problems. Knowledge is power, and these books, along with the five minutes of your introductory call free, are designed to help provide you, the reader, with the basic knowlege needed to protect those rights.

Contents

—

- Finding a decedent's assets and debts
- Finding beneficiaries
- Distributing estate money to beneficiaries and concluding a probate procedure

Introduction

———

A few years back, I was at a local bar having a couple of beers with some associates when the topic of estate planning came up. It's not that this is a popular subject among attorneys, even estate planning attorneys. In fact, contrary to how they make it appear on *L.A. Law*, when they have a break attorneys don't like to talk shop any more than anyone else, and let's face it, estate planning is, or at least can be, a depressing topic. It is, after all, planning for *death* or *disability*.

Nonetheless, the topic had arisen, and I was a little surprised to hear one of my associates (a personal injury attorney) announce that he had no Will, trust, or any form of an estate plan.

"Why should I?" he asked.

I replied in my most professional and concerned tone, "To ensure that your debts get paid, and your assets are distributed pursuant to your desires. You might also want to save on estate taxes and probate costs, and make things easier for your family and beneficiaries."

"Don't mean nothing to me," he said as he slugged down the rest of his beer.

"It doesn't mean anything to you." I corrected his English, then asked, "Why not?"

"I'll be dead."

Point well taken. He was a man of few (poorly chosen) words, but he had expressed something basic to the estate planning exercise: it is in no way mandatory. It is a matter of choice, of personal preference.

A person plans an estate because he or she cares about what happens after they die, and they have enough assets that a plan would make a difference. They care about who will get their property, the amount of hassle those people will have to go through, and the costs (taxes, probate, and others) they will need to pay to get it.

Not all people are like this, and the people who are vary in degree of concern and need, depending on family ties and amount of assets. A person with more debt than property may love his or her family, and be very concerned for their welfare should something happen, but have little need to do much in the way of an estate plan. Similarly, a person who has a whole pile of money but no concern over what happens to it after his or her death will have no use for creating an estate plan either.

In my legal associate's situation, he had a sizable estate, but disliked his kids—"leeches," he called them. His parents were dead, and he was divorced. Even worse, I think he just had a bad attitude (at that point) toward life. This, of course, was his right.

"What if you're disabled?" I questioned him. "You won't be dead, but you will be subject to the control of the court system, and maybe those young adult leeches. Shouldn't you do some estate planning for that?"

"I've got disability insurance," he answered, a little less certain now.

"That's a start, but who's going to determine how that money is spent for your care if you are unable to make decisions for yourself? Who will make decisions about your health care or your investments?"

"I never thought about that." He paused, thinking. "I guess my oldest son, Bob. He's the brightest of the lot."

"Well, if that's who you want, you'd better take steps to make sure that he has a form of durable power of attorney. Otherwise, it may be anyone the court appoints."

Estate plannning is as much planning for disability as for after death, and it doesn't have to be costly. In fact, compared to other areas of law, it may, overall, be the least expensive. Standard forms and self-help do-it-yourself books on estate planning subjects abound, making the law in this area very accessible to the average person.

Moreover, unlike divorce or other areas of the law where litigation and, often, dispute are parts of the process, estate planning only takes one to tango. You make all the decisions on what goals you want to achieve, how you will achieve them, and how much you will spend to do it, without the necessity of getting the consent, or even the opinion, of another.

An estate plan, or lack thereof, is in your control—all you have to do is understand the basics and ask the right questions. This book is designed to give you those basics and, by example, the questions most frequently asked by others concerned with estate planning issues.

Feel free to skip sections that seem meaningless to your personal goals. This is not a book where if you miss one section, the rest is incomprehensible. We will discuss general strategies and instruments in planning from the standpoint of what most people want to know. Maybe not all strategies or concerns, or all areas of the law—but the most frequently asked, and therefore, I assume, of the most interest to the average person.

This last part is important for you to understand before proceeding with this book. Estate planning is not a nice, neat, limited subject area of law, like divorce or bankruptcy. It borrows and pours over into many subject areas, like taxes, probate, wills, trusts, life insurance, and more. Thus, in the pages that follow, we will not even attempt to cover everything there is to know about estate planning—just the highlights.

This is an area of the law, however, that personifies, in my mind, the very important concept of Preventive Law, a concept developed by one of my former professors at USC Law School. It requires examining and taking care of your legal situation today, so that later—when you are unable to control the situation—events will unfold as you choose. It is a continual process of examining your concerns, goals, and needs, and planning accordingly.

For my associate, on that day, it was a limited plan for disability. Tomorrow, who knows? He could get remarried and have another kid—one whom he likes (you're never too old, they say)—or he could just make up with his existing kids. The world turns. . . .

It should also be noted that in some circles estate planning is not even considered an area of law. There are, for your enlightenment, nonattorney estate planners trained and ready to offer you advice and sell you estate planning products (also known as investments) like life insurance, mutual funds, annuities, and even living trusts. We will discuss these products to the extent they relate to frequently asked questions on this subject, but our obvious slant will be toward the legal implications of what they mean, rather than the financial.

In short, this book will offer you a potpourri of information concerning the estate planning decision process from a legal standpoint. Questions like: Should I have a will and/or a living trust? What can a power of attorney do, and what doesn't it do? Can life insurance save taxes?

These questions, and many others, are examined in the pages that follow. Combined with the happy accounts and horror stories of those that planned and those that didn't plan for their disability and/or death, it should provide you with the basic information you need, in an easy-to-read and understandable format, so that you can make the individual choice of how much and what you will do (if anything) in creating your own estate plan.

CHAPTER ONE

Estate Planning Goals

As we saw by example in the introduction, you have to care about something in order to feel the need to set up a plan for its future. With my associate, he did not care about his estate after his death, but he did care about it while he was alive in case he ever became disabled. Everyone has their own desires and needs, and before you start to plan, you need to identify yours.

Maybe it's making sure your minor children are cared for; or that a certain person doesn't get their hands on any of your money; or even that your family gets your assets with a minimum of fuss and cost; or maybe it's a combination of these or other things. Whatever it is, before you can start your estate plan, you need to establish what it is you want. You need to establish your goals.

Generally, there are four estate planning goals: (1) avoiding probate; (2) assuring proper distribution of property after death; (3) avoiding taxes; and (4) providing for disability. As we pose strategy solutions to the questions that follow, see if you can identify which of these goals the questioner is trying to meet.

What Can Be Done to Save Costs in the Processing of a Will?

This is the big one, the big goal, for most people: avoiding probate—saving costs. Probate is the process by which property is transferred from the decedent's estate to the beneficiaries. The decedent is the person who has died and whose property is being transferred. The beneficiaries are the person or persons who are to receive the property.

When a person dies, his or her property has to go somewhere, so, by law, it temporarily goes into something we've been referring to as an "estate." An estate is an artificial entity created to hold assets when the owner can't. Probate is the court process created to handle and wind up the affairs of a decedent's estate, ultimately by transferring the assets held in the estate to the beneficiaries (and/or creditors).

If you stop to think about it, you see how easy and logical the system is. When you die, you cannot act for yourself. Your Will tells the people you leave behind what you want to happen, but you need someone to carry those instructions out. That person is an executor or personal representative. The court is around to make sure this executor follows your instructions and the law.

An executor, as we shall later see in more detail, makes sure the decedent's investments and businesses are taken care of or sold, if needed, that debts are paid, and that the remaining assets are distributed as the decedent specified in the Will. This is the probate process.

So what's wrong with this? Why does almost every estate plan have as its center the avoidance of probate?

The answer is simple: the cost, and time delays.

Probate, although now streamlined in many states, is still generally a slow, paper intensive, expensive procedure. You must file the right documents at the right time. You need to notify creditors and wait for their responses. And you need to pay a personal representative and maybe an attorney to handle the process.

Of course, to the extent *you* means the decedent, you don't have to do anything—since you are dead. It's the people left behind that are forced to arrange for all this cleanup. It can be an arduous task, and is better avoided as a general policy.

Much of this book will address in one form or another ways to avoid probate. We will have examples of trusts and bank accounts—commonly called "pay-on-death" accounts—that can do this; we will also see how to avoid probate by making gifts during your lifetime and holding title in the form of joint tenancy with rights of survivorship. These are just a few of the options. Keep in mind, however, that in some situations you may want to insist a probate process proceed. For example:

> **I want to leave my estate to my wife and six children. She is my second wife, and the mother of only my two youngest daughters. My other kids have never really accepted her and there has been some nasty fighting between them. For a long time I had hoped to get them all together, but I've given up trying as of late. I'm afraid if I die there will be fighting over my property and I would like to avoid that. The estate planners I have spoken with have suggested that I avoid probate and set up a trust, but I can't—for business reasons—put all my property in a trust. What can you suggest?**

If there is truly no way to use a trust, and there are several situations when you can't, then you're back to doing a basic Will, which means probate. But in this type of situation—especially with so many people involved—a probate procedure with an independent referee may be just the thing to ensure that your desires are followed and a fair distribution of the estate occurs. The important thing is to make the Will as specific as possible in designating who gets what, and to try to select a fair, impartial personal representative to handle the probate, preferably one who is not a beneficiary and has no ties with either side of the potential dispute.

How Can I Ensure That the People I Want to Leave My Property to, Get It?

This question is far too easy to be the real question in the mind of the typical person who asks it—you simply write up a Will or trust which sets forth how you want your property distributed.

Chances are, however, that a person who asks this type of question really has a semihidden agenda involving making sure a certain person or persons do not get control or ownership of the property. An example of this is:

> **I have three children from a former marriage to whom I would like to leave property, but two of them are still under age and will be for some time. I'm afraid if I leave them property, my ex-wife will get her hands on it, and there won't be anything left for them when they are old enough to make their own decisions.**

This kind of problem cries out for what is sometimes called "dead hand control." It's a term we will see applied in many situations in estate planning and simply means what it suggests: limitations placed on the receipt of a gift by the decedent.

For situations such as those posed in this example, there are several options, mainly through a Will or trust, each of which involves some form of limiting language, or dead hand control, on access to the property. Several of these options and devises will be discussed in greater detail in Chapter 3 on Wills, Chapter 4 on trusts, and Chapter 8 in the section on gifts to minors. For now, it is important to note only that the goal of ensuring proper distribution of one's estate is a basic goal, which can be achieved through limiting language in the proper documents of transfer.

What's the Best Way to Avoid Conflict Between Estate Beneficiaries?

The only honest answer to this question is: I wish I knew. Each situation is unique, and there seems to be no guaranteed way to keep beneficiaries away from each other's throats. On the other hand, one formula for *creating* conflict—often pointed out by estate planning attorneys in meetings with their clients—is to give similar beneficiaries —children, for example, unequal shares. The one getting the lesser share commonly feels cheated and will look for a reason to fight.

This, unfortunately, doesn't mean that giving similar beneficiaries equal shares will avoid all fighting. In such a situation, one of the persons may feel more "deserving," and want to challenge any gift given to the other. A recent situation I handled for an independent paralegal friend of mine in Los Angeles is illustrative.

An elderly woman in her nineties, not in the best of health, came to my friend—who was also the elderly woman's niece—and asked for help in making a Will. My friend did as she was requested, providing some specific gifts to certain persons, but basically dividing the estate equally between all of the woman's nieces and nephews. It was a simple Will, and, I noted, well constructed. It also provided for the disinheritance of the woman's elderly sister, who at the time was in even worse health than the woman herself, and it required certain of the nieces and nephews to accept a deduction for money they had received from the aunt previously.

About a month after making this Will, the woman's health turned from bad to very, very bad, and she went into the hospital. Shortly thereafter, another niece, one from New York, flew out to Los Angeles, where the woman was in the hospital, and had her released. The hospital records showed that the woman was in extremely poor condition at the time, mentioning in several places that she was "confused" and "disoriented." The doctor mentioned that she was released "with no expectation of recovery," and only upon the insistence of the niece, who had told the doctor that she was the woman's only living relative.

The niece from New York then hired an attorney to draft a trust for the woman. It named the niece trustee and changed the distribution of the estate from what was contained in the earlier Will. She also got herself placed on several bank accounts as joint holder.

The woman died about four days later and all hell broke loose as the eight nieces and nephews vied to take sides. The niece who was named as trustee locked everything up and started cleaning out bank accounts—which was about the time my paralegal friend brought me into the case.

The attorney who drafted the trust was extremely nice about the whole thing (and well he should have been, from what we found), explaining that he had met with the decedent and she seemed to understand what was going on when she signed the trust. When I asked him why a woman who had just drafted a Will a month earlier would decide to change the distribution and the form, he had no answer. In fact, he was unaware of the Will's existence. I also noted to him that her signature on the trust was rather shaky (that was putting it nicely: the signature was unreadable), and he again had no answer except that she appeared, to him, to be competent.

I, the medical records, and my paralegal friend respectfully disagreed with his assessment of her competence, and negotiations to work out the differences between the parties began.

As far as the attorneys were concerned, it was a matter of competence and settlement. Was she competent enough to sign on the trust or not? If not, then it was invalid and the earlier Will controlled the distribution of her property. If she was competent, then the trust controlled the property to be distributed.

Recognizing this, we had two options: litigation before the probate court to determine the decedent's competence at the time she signed the trust, or settlement on some compromise solution with everyone's—all beneficiaries'—agreement. Obviously, the second alternative was the less costly and risky from the perspective of both sides, but not necessarily the easier.

Settlement discussions took us into a small conference room where the two key parties, the niece from New York and my client, sat across the table from each other refusing to make eye contact. These women, who were first cousins and had once played together as kids—but never liked each other, as they were both quick to point out—were now on the edge of battle over money that wasn't even theirs.

The attorney for the New York cousin spoke first, and focused the meeting on solving the dispute quickly and fairly. In this he was generally successful, as all the issues except one were solved before the meeting was complete, and a plan was devised as to how to come to a solution on the final issue. The plan involved seeking the intervention of a rabbinical tribunal, the idea being that the tribunal could make the final decision after hearing both sides, without going to court. Given the parties' Jewish faith, it seemed like a reasonable solution to the problem.

When all seemed resolved and the nastiness avoided, the question arose as to where to find the rabbis—which then led to the question of which temple their aunt (the deceased) had attended services at. One cousin said one temple, the other said another, and that started a battle to prove who knew—and was loved by—the aunt best. They quizzed each other back and forth, describing their close moments with their aunt, and how the other could care less about her.

"She stayed with me last year in New York over the holidays," the New York cousin said.

"She came to our house regularly and we went to hers," countered the Los Angeles cousin.

"I bet you don't even know her birthday."

"I do so—August tenth. And I was with her on her last birthday. Where were you?"

And so on and so forth. The meeting was over—only the bitterness was left. How do you stop this from happening in the first place? It may be nearly impossible when someone is willing to go as far as the New York cousin did in this example. However, in a more typical situation, you might try telling your beneficiaries about your chosen distribution before you die (this is often not easy—emotionally or otherwise), so that they will understand your thinking on the matter. You should also try to draft clear language in your estate documents to avoid any misinterpretations that may be used to create a battle. You can also add a provision, standard in many Wills, that disinherits anyone who challenges the Will—though it wouldn't have worked in this case.

In the end, however, you can only hope everyone is reasonable. Anyone can challenge a Will, or do things that may appear sneaky or deceptive, especially when the decedent is ill and helpless for a period of time just prior to death. That is not to say that they cannot justify their acts, as the New York cousin was quick to do.

"I was only protecting her estate, and in any case, I was her closest relative."

Everyone feels justified in these cases and feels that the other side is undeserving. To borrow from another cliché: Equal and fair are in the eye of the beholder.

What Can Be Done to Ensure That the Inheritance Is Used Wisely (or in a Way That You Think Is Right)?

This is another one of those questions that, at the heart, are really about dead hand control. You're giving a sum of money to your kids or spouse, who may never have had money, and you're concerned that they will lose it on some crazy investment, or spend it without thinking; or maybe you are concerned that the money will go to their heads; or maybe you have a concern like this person's:

> **I'm getting on in years and would like to leave what I have to my wife and kids if something happens to me. Part of what I have is a farm in Nebraska, which my family has owned for the last three generations, and which I would hope my children would continue to retain in the family. The only thing is that they have all gone into other careers and really know nothing about farming. Is there anything I can do to ensure it stays in the family for my grandchildren?**

Complicated as this request is, it still comes down to the testator (the person making the Will) wanting to set limits or controls on the use or distribution of property made as a gift after his death. In this case, he wants to keep certain property in the family. In other cases the person wants to make sure that the property can be used only for certain things, such as school or religious purposes, or that it cannot be used for others, like to sell alcohol.

These are all legitimate requests based on a legitimate goal: to limit access to or control over gifted property. However, the law in this area is tricky. So tricky, in fact, that in some cases courts have held that even attorneys cannot be expected to fully understand the law. The problem is that certain property laws restrict how much and how long a person can control a property's use and ownership after death, especially if the control affects the marketability of the property—which it almost always does.

We will touch on this subject again in later chapters. For now, it's important only to note that while the goal of restraining use or disposition of transferred property is legitimate, it may be restricted by local law. It would therefore behoove you to seek expert advice from a real specialist, if you're planning to do anything extraordinary along this line.

What Can Be Done to Save on Taxes?

This is the most misunderstood area of estate planning, partially because the complexity of the tax law almost always causes misunderstanding and confusion, and partially because of misinformation passed around by unscrupulous or uninformed salespersons wanting to sell estate planning instruments—a trust or life insurance. However, there is no reason for you, after reading this book, to be ignorant about or make a mistake on what tax benefits you can and cannot achieve—as you will see here and in Chapter 9.

Taxes are an important part of an estate plan. Generally, when we talk about saving taxes, we are talking about *estate* taxes, rather than *income* taxes or some other type of tax you are more used to (although these other taxes can play a part in the planning process).

Estate taxes are taxes based on what is referred to as a "gross estate," or the total of all the decedent's *assets* at the time of death, not the decedent's *income* over a period of time. The aim of the law is to tax property transferred at death. Generally, this includes property held in trust as well as that given outright by a Will.

The reason for trying to minimize taxes when planning an estate may appear obvious, but there are less obvious subtleties that need to be considered, as shown by the following situation:

My mother died last month and my sister and I are trying to get her estate in order. My father died last year, leaving her everything he had, and now she has left it all to us. It is quite a sizable estate, including several apartment houses and a commercial warehouse. All the properties bring in regular rental income, and, in total, may be worth between $1.5 and $1.7 million. Our accountant tells us that there will be substantial estate taxes—nearly $300,000, but my mother had cash assets of only about $100,000, much of which we have already spent. What can we do?

Having insufficient cash to pay estate taxes is not an uncommon problem. Over a lifetime a person or couple amass a lot of assets, many of which are not liquid (cannot be easily sold and turned into cash). This can create a problem similar to the situation above. Dealing with this problem would have been much easier if it had been planned by the parents from the start, rather than being dealt with by the daughters after their deaths. They could have, for example, set up a special marital (A-B) trust, discussed in Chapter 4, which would have reduced this tax by almost $200,000, and then made annual gifts to further reduce the tax. Or they could have bought life insurance to provide the liquidity (cash) to pay the tax.

The point, for now, is that taxes can have "taxing" (excuse the pun, I couldn't help myself) effects beyond the simple cost of the tax. The woman in this situation does not have the cash to pay the tax, which means she and her sister will have to sell off one of the property holdings to get the money. This is, in a sense, a forced sale, which means that the price they will likely get will not be the optimum. They have lost the choice of examining the market and waiting for the right buyer. They may be forced to accept the first bid that comes through the door. Or worse, in a very slow market, they may not get a reasonable offer and have to auction the property off to pay the estate taxes. If they don't do it, the IRS may do it for them.

Can Income Taxes Be Saved as Part of an Estate Plan?

You should also note that saving *income* taxes is often a goal of an estate plan. For example, as most of us know, there is an income tax to be paid on the sale of an asset that has appreciated in value, such as one's home. This is calculated by subtracting the "basis" of the property (generally the cost at the time of purchase) from the net sales price and multiplying by the applicable tax rate. Thus, if you bought a house for $50,000, then sold it for $150,000 (net of any costs of sale) and were in the 28 percent tax bracket, you would pay a tax of $28,000 ($150,000 − 50,000 = $100,000 × .28 = $28,000).

But what happens if the person who owns the property does not sell it, and so continues to own it at the time he or she dies? A magical thing happens, via the tax law: there is a step-up in the basis. This means that the basis is increased to the value of the property at the time of the decedent's death (or alternative valuation date). Thus, in our example in the last paragraph, if the home owner died when the house was worth $150,000, the basis of the property would step up to $150,000. If the heir then turned around and sold the house for this amount, no tax would be owed ($150,000 − $150,000 = 0 × .28 = 0).

We will discuss this more fully in Chapter 9, but the value of this step-up to the planning process is evident. A piece of property that has greatly increased in value may be better held until after death rather than sold, when any income tax gains can be wiped out by the step-up in basis.

What Can Be Done to Plan for Disability or Incapacity?

In many ways, the planning goals dealing with death and those dealing with disability are very similar. As in death, disability means being unable to do for yourself and needing others to oversee your affairs. In any case, disability is no less an important planning target than death, as the following question indicates:

> My father recently had a stroke, and the doctors say he will be out of it for several months, if he ever fully recovers. He owns a half interest in a medium-size machine shop, which I believe needs to be watched while he is incapacitated. I spoke to his partner, but he says he doesn't need to recognize me, and frankly I'm a little concerned. What can I, or my mother, do at this point?

Whatever it is, it won't be as simple as it would have been if his father had given him a durable power of attorney to act on his behalf before he became disabled. As you probably guessed, after a stroke or other disabling event during which a person's mental capacities are diminished, he cannot authorize someone to act on his behalf, simply because he is not competent to do so. The key test is whether the person understands the nature and extent of what he is doing.

If this questioner's father does not have this capacity, then it would likely take a court order appointing the son (or wife) as conservator of his estate—pending recovery—

to force the partner to deal with him as he would the father.

A good disability plan considers two important issues: finances and health. The issue of finances, as seen in this example, is basically who will make the decisions and how will these decisions be made regarding the business and financial affairs of the disabled person.

The health issues, similarly, are who will make the decisions and how will they be made regarding the health care of the disabled person. Neither is more important than the other, and both should be handled before the disabling event. We will, in the chapters that follow, have occasion to see examples and discuss several important points regarding both of these disability issues.

CHAPTER TWO

Documents and Forms

A somewhat paranoid attorney once said to me, "We've got to stop all these forms. Standardization will be the death of the law. Soon anyone will be able to handle their own legal affairs because all they'll have to do is fill out a form—and then where will we be?" Actually, he was a little drunk at the time, as well as paranoid, but there is a segment of the legal profession that does fear standardization, and a much larger segment of the general population that craves—no, demands—more of it.

And well they should. A form document, when it exists or can be created, is a great way to access the protection of the law. Indeed, attorneys have used standard forms almost since the beginning of the practice of law, they just haven't made them available to the general public—except when selling their services.

I remember my first year as an attorney being asked to draft a Will and a quitclaim deed by one of the firm's senior partners. I accepted the project, of course, and then set out for the law library to do what I thought was the necessary research. About two hours into the assignment, another attorney at the firm, an older and—I thought at the time—wiser attorney, chanced by and asked what I was working on so feverishly.

"Doing some research."

"Research? What for?" he asked incredulously.

"I was asked to draft a Will and a deed."

"So, I repeat: research, what for?" He smiled an all-knowing smile, which I remember kind of irked me at the time. I was unsure of how to reply to that smile, but luckily I didn't have to. He continued: "Why not just go to the form files?"

"Form files, what are those?" I remember thinking how intriguing that sounded. He told me about a certain partner with the firm that kept the sacred Will form files and another that kept the sacred deed form files. It was like learning a secret handshake during the initiation into a mysterious underground club.

"The form files have it all," he announced with confidence. "Go through it and find the one that fits your situation, and use it."

I must admit I was very excited to have learned this secret. It had great promise. No research meant less work, and less work meant—well, we all know what that means. Moreover, using a partner's form meant less risk. It had already stood the test of time and had been approved by the powers that be. How could I lose?

As he left, he turned back to me and added the following bit of advice: "Just remember, don't f°%! with the forms."

I understood immediately what his warning entailed: Don't change the language in the forms. It seemed logical. They were, after all, the *forms.* So I went, as he suggested, to the senior partner's secretary and, showing no surprise at my request, she showed me where the form files were located.

The first thing that struck me was the thickness of the files. This was just before the age of computers made such hard copies meaningless, and there were hundreds of different deeds in one, and hundreds of different Wills in the other. The second thing that struck me was that these weren't forms at all—at least, not the type where you fill in the blanks. These were samples of documents actually used for different people and different situations.

A little thought put me in conflict: how was I supposed to be true to these samples (not "f°%! with the forms") and still draft a Will and a deed for the situation I had been assigned? What made the whole thing more difficult was that my Will involved a gift to a *cat,* which, at the time, seemed anything but standard.

I rummaged through hundreds of samples (I might as well have done the research) looking for a Will that transferred assets to a cat (or any animal, for that matter), but couldn't find one. In desperation I began to piece together several samples and fill in my own language, attempting to make the bequests requested by the client fit into the format provided. In the end it seemed to flow and make sense, but, then again, the risk had returned. This was not a standardized preapproved form. It was something drafted to fit the client's need, which included my language and interpretation of what the partner had said she wanted. I had, in effect, "f°%!ed with the forms."

I was thus very pleasantly surprised when the partner came back to me raving about the job I had done. Apparently, creative writing was not typical among attorneys in the office—or among attorneys in general—and this had impressed him no end. He made two small changes and I was off to a career.

The incident taught me a few things about the practice of law. First, standard forms—the kind where you simply fill in the blanks—are nice when you can get them because they save time and avoid mistakes, but they are not always available or applicable to every situation. Second, when they do not exist, there are still samples, always samples. Someone else has almost certainly done what you want to do. It may not have been the exact same situation, but it was close. All you need to do is to find that sample and adapt it to your situation. It only takes a little creative writing and some basic common sense.

Finally, the most important thing I learned was that a lawyer who wants to represent his client's best interests will always f°%! with the forms. Without that, what has he really done? Copied a few documents, changing the names. The value of a lawyer's service in documentation is being able to tailor the text to the needs of the client.

What you will find as you read on is that these sample documents and standardized forms are readily available to you, the average person, at least as they concern estate planning instruments. They come on computer disks or in print, and include virtually everything you will need to do your own estate plan. If you are not good at writing, or even at filling in the blanks of forms, there are also people available to help do this at a reasonable cost. As this is a major part of the estate planning process, the area is far more accessible to the average person than you might realize. All you need to decide is what you want to do. I believe this book will help you decide by answering those questions that are most frequently asked in this area of law.

What Kind of Documents Are Used in an Estate Plan?

As suggested above, almost every document you would need for a complete estate plan is available as a sample or standardized form. The only question—and it's a big one —is which form you will need for your particular plan. We can start by identifying which documents are available to an estate planner.

The most obvious and well-known estate planning document is a Will. A Will is an instrument that purports to give instructions on how your assets will be distributed and your debts repaid following your death. It is quite literally a reflection of your will (desire), which you wish to be carried out by others because you cannot do so yourself.

The good news is that sample Wills and even statutory Will forms are plentiful and available everywhere. They come in:

(1) <u>single or two-page forms</u> with fill-in-the-blank parts and simple instructions, available in stationery stores for a few dollars;

(2) <u>self-help books</u> with more detailed instructions and options on what can be done and provisions that can be used (less fill-in-the-blanks, more creative writing), sold at book stores for about fifteen to twenty dollars or available in libraries;

(3) <u>computer programs</u> designed to ask you questions, and in the end spit out a neat and complete Will ready for signing, sold at book and computer/software stores for about fifty to seventy-five dollars; and

(4) <u>legal form books</u> developed for attorneys, with more detailed descriptions of the law surrounding the document, available in law libraries (and for sale from law book distributors—but you have to buy the entire form book, which generally will contain hundreds of other documents and cost several hundred dollars).

Another key estate planning document is the trust. A trust is simply a way to hold and maintain property. Legal title to the trust property is held by a trustee, who holds it for the benefit of—and is responsible to—a beneficiary who has "equitable title" to the property. A little more complicated than Wills (but not much, as we shall see), sample trusts are just as available, and for about the same prices as shown for Wills above. Note, however, there are several different varieties of trusts, each performing a different legal trick. Thus, before you go shopping around for a trust, you will want to determine which type you need (see Chapter 4).

A power of attorney is another document that is used in planning an estate, largely for disability purposes, since it becomes ineffective upon the death of the provider of the power. It is generally a designation of one person to act in the stead of the giver of the power, in his or her name, as if they were that person. Thus, a holder of a power of attorney can sign documents and make decisions about the property owned by another person (more on this later), but only while they're alive.

Documents creating a power of attorney are even simpler than those that create Wills or trusts. Usually contained in a one-page form (with instructions) they can be found in all the locations described above for Wills. Keep in mind that what you will often be looking for in this area of estate planning is a special type of power of attorney, called a "durable" or "springing" power of attorney. These types of powers do not typically take effect until the giver of the power becomes disabled or is unable to make his or her own decisions. Thus, such a power is said to spring up at the time of the disability, or is durable in that it survives the occurrence of the disability. If this is what you are looking for, you will need to check the forms carefully to make sure they can handle this (as well as state law, to make sure it allows this).

Another less used but also simple document in this area is the so-called living will. The name conjures up images of a cross between a living trust and a Will, and is often confused by clients with one or the other of these instruments. In fact, it is nothing like either; it's simply a request to one's relatives, doctor, lawyer, and clergy to be taken off life support and allowed to die naturally if ever totally incapacitated and kept alive by artificial means without any reasonable chance of recovery. I suppose the term *living will* makes some sense, since it is like a Will in that it gives instructions on what you want, only it applies while you are still alive—albeit in a limited way. In order to avoid confusion, many lawyers will refer to such a document as a pull-the-plug provision (for obvious reasons).

Living will forms may be found in all the same places as Wills, living trusts, and powers of attorney. They are usually half a page long and may even be found as add-ons to a Will program or kit.

Also used as an integral part of estate planning are deeds. Deeds are instruments of transfer for real property. They come in various forms, such as quitclaim and warranty deed, but they are basically the document used to convey property from one person to another.

Like most of the other documents we have discussed in this section, deeds are readily available, with instructions, in simple one-page forms.

One thing to note, however, is that deeds typically involve recordation with a county recorder's office. This means that the forms must comply with the local standards of that recorder. If you are unsure, you should always check with the local authorities in the county where the property is located to ensure the general deed form you intend to use will be accepted for filing.

Estate planning also includes things like life insurance and pay-on-death accounts. The forms for setting up these items are provided by the life insurance companies and banks that offer them. More on this later.

Where Can I Find Probate Forms?

Unfortunately, forms and documents for handling a probate are not so readily available or as easily put together as the documents we have just discussed—which is another reason you want to avoid probate. The good news is that most states have simplified their probate procedures of late, making them relatively easy and less formal. Some states even provide alternative short form probate procedures, or exemptions for small estates.

The bad news is that probate procedures, even without a dispute, can still be a nasty maze of forms, notice requirements, and time limits. More on this in Chapter 10.

If you're lucky, you live in a state where someone has published a self-help book, including forms, on how to do your own probate. Such a book should take you through an entire probate procedure, using simple English and sample forms. Try calling several bookstores to see whether any such books are available in your area.

As an alternative, you can always pick up forms from your local probate court, to the extent these forms exist. Probate court is usually a section or department of the local superior, circuit, or district court, but may come under other court names like the Supreme Court or Court of Common Pleas.

Once you find the right court, you will be able to get all the basic forms available from the clerk's office. Hopefully these will be all the forms you need to handle the probate, but if not, you may have to seek out those legal form files at your local law library (see page 24). You can also go through actual court records—they are, after all, *public* records—for samples of what attorneys have filed in other probate proceedings. These samples can be copied, modified, and adapted to fit your needs.

Barring access to such forms and samples, your only option is to seek outside help in preparing and filing the proper forms.

Where Can I Find Help with the Preparation of Estate Planning Documents?

For those who don't have time for all this self-help stuff, or who aren't good with forms but are stuck with having to handle a probate, there is help available from two outside sources: independent paralegals, and attorneys.

Independent paralegals (IPs) are persons who are knowledgeable and experienced—sometimes self-trained—in certain basic legal procedures and how to prepare legal forms and documents. Obviously, you want to seek the help of someone whose experience is in the area you need help with: that is, probate, Wills, or trusts, for the purposes we have discussed in this book. For probate help, make sure that the person is familiar with the courts and procedures in your local area, or you may be paying for them to learn what you could have done on your own.

IPs can be excellent for doing the basic paper pushing that needs to be done in the probate process—filing the petition for probate and the notices and other documents involved. In many cases that is all there is. IPs, however, are limited in what they can do, even if they know more, by unauthorized practice of law statutes that apply in almost every state. These laws, to the extent they are clear (most are fairly vague), limit unlicensed personnel—nonattorneys—from giving legal advice and practicing law. Most would not, however, prohibit filling in forms (a typing service) as directed by the client, or providing help in the filing of the documents. If you need help beyond this, you will have to seek the advice or help of a licensed attorney. In many states, you may not be able to avoid using an attorney because the court rules require one in some manner.

There are basically two ways an attorney is compensated for probate work: on a per-hour basis, or with a percentage of the estate. Either way, they take charge of much of what happens during the probate, and are subject only to the contrary instruction of the executor or personal representative.

Another approach is to hire an attorney, at a fixed cost (say $250), to do specific things you cannot do yourself in the probate—for example, make two court appearances. The trouble is finding attorneys who are willing to work with you in this manner. If you can, however, you will gain greater control and save costs in the process. You will also take on a greater portion of the responsibility for what happens. It's a personal choice of how much you want to get involved.

CHAPTER THREE

Wills

What Happens if You Don't Have a Will?

Everyone needs a Will, or so they say. But did you ever wonder what happens if you don't have one? A lot of people don't, and have called to ask. The most interesting of these calls, however, are the people who are beyond the stage of wondering and are in the middle of experiencing the effects of not having a Will. For example:

> My husband just died in a car accident. He had some life insurance, but no Will or anything like that. He was always afraid that if he wrote a Will,

he would be signing his death warrant. We had no
kids together, but he did have a little girl from his
first marriage. She's now eleven. Her mother has
asked some questions regarding what we own, and
it has me concerned. Does she have a claim
against our property?

or

I have a wealthy first cousin who just died. He was
divorced and had no children. His parents are
both dead and so are my parents, his uncle and
aunt. I think I am the next of kin. If he doesn't
have a Will, and no one has been able to find one,
do I inherit his money?

When someone dies with a Will, they die "testate,"
and the Will—barring a successful challenge—determines
where the property goes. These questions focus our attention on the opposite situation, when a person dies without
a Will, or dies "intestate."

Who decides the distribution of the property of a
person who dies intestate? The simple answer is that the
law—ultimately a court—decides by what we commonly
call the rules of "intestate succession" or "consanguinity."
These rules are based on kinship or blood relationships.

For this purpose, the law—in the form of a statute or
court decisions—usually sets up a hierarchy of family relationships in which property passes to what the questioner
above refers to as the "next of kin." While this hierarchy
may change slightly from state to state, there is a surprising amount of consistency. Refer to your own state law for
specifics, but here is what you will generally find:

(1) First in line to inherit are the spouse and children. This includes natural as well as adopted children, and even illegitimate children, but does not typically include stepchildren. Ex-spouses are also excluded.

—If there is a spouse, but no children, the spouse will get it all.
—If there are children, but no spouse, the children get it all (split equally among them).
—If there are children and a spouse, they split the property, sometimes fifty-fifty, sometimes one third–two thirds in favor of the kids, with the kids splitting their portion equally among themselves.

Keep in mind that what gets divided is only the property of the decedent (the person who died). Thus, in the case of a husband and wife, the portion of property that is owned by the surviving spouse goes to that spouse without division with the children. Whether particular property is owned by one spouse or the other, or is somehow shared between them, is determined by local property law and so may vary from state to state. This is especially true in states that have enacted community property laws. Community property states often provide that all community property goes to the surviving spouse regardless of whether there are children. If you are interested in this topic, see Chapter 7 on joint tenancy, where the "right of survivorship" automatically gives the decedent's share to the surviving co-owner(s).

(2) Next in line are the grandchildren and great-grandchildren, or "issue": persons who are in what is called the "line of succession." The order is again determined by closest blood relationship—grandchildren before great-grandchildren, and so on—but if someone on one level of blood relationship has died earlier, his or her decedents may still take by "right of representation" (often referred to as *per stirpes*). For example, assuming there are no children or a spouse, if there are three great-grandchildren, two from one of the decedent's grandchildren and one from another, they don't split the estate evenly. The two from the one parent get half to split, and the other one gets the other half. Note, however, that this can change from state to state and situation to situation.

(3) After the issue, the rules take us up and out on the decedent's family chart. First, up to the parents of the decedent, then out to the decedent's brothers and sisters (and later to their children, the nieces and nephews). When these family members have been exhausted, we go up again to the grandparents, then out to the uncles and aunts (then later to their children, the cousins). Generally, if you look on the chart on page 36, you can find the next of kin by counting the number of levels the person is from the decedent, moving up and

out along the family tree. The closest relative wins the inheritance lottery.

This gives us enough information to answer the questions provided above. As to the widow and her husband's daughter from the first marriage, they will probably split his estate between them (which may be what he wanted anyway—maybe not). A difficult question posed here is who does the widow, as executor of the estate, deal with when it comes to the inheritance of the eleven-year-old girl? The obvious choice will be the girl's mother, as guardian, who could protect and handle the inheritance until the child became of age (this might not be something the decedent wanted). The parents, even though they are alive, would probably get nothing (this may also be something he didn't want).

Before this split, however, it is important to note that her share of property that was owned by both her and her husband before his death will go to her, and in some situations all shares of the property will go to her, being jointly held property with a right of survivorship.

As to our second question, we can go to our chart (or better yet to the rules of intestate succession in the caller's state) and see he's probably the next of kin who gets the inheritance. He tells us that there is no wife, no kids, no parents, and no aunts or uncles—his parents, if he is a first cousin. Assuming there are no grandchildren or other issue, and no brothers or sisters, or nieces or nephews, he and the other first cousins, if any, would be the ones to inherit.

Note that other than choosing the heirs, the probate process without a Will is largely the same as with a Will.

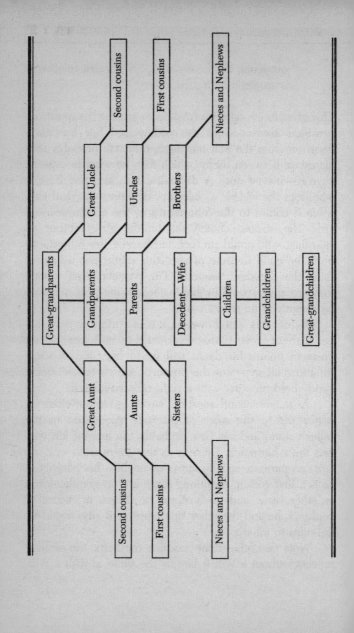

Many of the same documents are filed, the executor/personal representative is appointed, the assets are gathered and bills are paid, and the heirs are given what remains, all under court supervision.

All this may bring you to the conclusion that my original statement—everyone needs a Will—is incorrect. Someone who wanted his or her property to pass exactly as the rules of intestate succession designate could forget about making a Will and just let the law handle the distribution. There are, however, other issues to take into account before dismissing the benefits of a Will. For example, with a Will you can decide on and appoint the person who will be your executor, and free him or her from the legal obligation of posting a bond. Without a Will, a judge chooses your executor and the law may require him to post a bond—to ensure he doesn't steal the property and properly performs his responsibilities.

Consider also the situation of the decedent in our first question. He may have wanted his estate to be split between his wife and little girl, but he may not have wanted his first wife to have any control of it. A Will would have given him the ability to keep that from happening.

To sum up, we are talking about control. Control over what will happen to your assets after you die. It is the reason why every estate planning and probate attorney I know advises all his clients to make a Will, no matter how poor they are. If you don't care about where it goes or who makes that decision, then you're probably one of the few people who really don't need a Will.

What Must Be in a Will?

People are always asking questions like: How many witnesses do I need? Does the Will need to be filed somewhere? Can it be handwritten? Does it need blue cardboard backing on it? In short, questions regarding format — What does a Will need to look like to be legal?

State laws in this regard are remarkably similar and generally simple. Here are the basic requirements to make a Will legal, after which you can pretty much do anything you like:

(1) The person making the Will must be a legal adult (eighteen years of age in most states).

(2) The person making the Will must be of sound mind.

(3) The Will must be typewritten or off a printer, except in states that accept holographic Wills.

(4) The Will must be dated, distribute at least some property, and appoint an executor.

(5) The Will must be signed in front of three witnesses (in some states only two) who cannot inherit under the Will (some states do not require this), are aware that it's a Will being signed and who actually witness the signing (they do not need to read the Will or know its contents). In some states, the decedent can direct another person to sign for him or her in front of witnesses, under limited circumstances.

The following are some common questions illustrating misconceptions of how a Will must be set up.

Do I Need to Notarize My Will?

There is no requirement that a Will be notarized, recorded, or filed anywhere—there is no place to file it anyway. However, in some states when a Will is notarized—sometimes referred to as a "self-proving" Will—it can avoid the need for affidavits from witnesses at a probate hearing.

Can I Handwrite My Will?

In about half the states a handwritten Will—also called a holographic Will—may be accepted by a probate court. It must be completely handwritten by the person making the Will, and there are no witnesses needed when this is allowed. Holographic Wills are often more suspect as to authenticity, are poorly written and hard to understand. They should thus be written only in an emergency situation, and exchanged for a more formal typewritten Will as soon as the emergency has ended.

Can I Videotape My Will?

You can, but don't rely on it alone. A videotaped Will is not admissible into probate, and so cannot be used as a substitute for a fully executed and written Will. The value of a videotape is that it can be used as evidence of the decedent's competence or to show that he wasn't subject to undue influence at the time he made the Will—thus avoiding a potential Will conflict.

What's Involved in the Process of Making a Will?

Most attorneys like to start by getting a current inventory of the person's assets and debts. You can do this yourself by simply taking a piece of paper, drawing a line down the middle, and listing assets in the left column and debts in the right. Assets include everything you own, whether tangible like your house and car or intangible like stocks and life insurance. Debts include everything you owe, whether it's secured by an asset like a house mortgage or unsecured like a typical credit card debt. You should include it all, and update the list on a regular basis.

The next thing to do is to create a list of beneficiaries, people you want to give something to if you die tomorrow, and, to a lesser extent, people you want to make sure get nothing. As discussed in the section on disinheritance (see page 46), you probably need to list only children and/or a spouse, if this is your intent. The rest of the family can be disinherited just by ignoring them in the Will.

With these lists completed, you are ready to start drafting the Will. The first thing to do is to name the executor or personal representative. This is the person who will administer the estate and make the financial decisions for you after you're dead. Obviously, you'll want to choose someone who you trust to be fair and honest with the handling of your assets, and who is most likely to follow your intentions.

Moreover, it may make sense to pick someone who is not an heir under the Will, so that he or she can be impartial during the probate process. This is not necessary if there is only one heir, or if you feel comfortable that everyone will get along with the decisions of the person you put in charge. Keep in mind, however, that more than one family relationship has been soured by the decision of an executor-heir which was perceived as unfair by the other beneficiaries under the Will.

In line with choosing an executor, you will want to lay out his or her authority, and any requirements for acting as the executor. Note that many standard Will forms give an executor broad authority in order to preserve the estate, and release him or her from the obligation to post a bond, which might otherwise be required. These types of provisions, unless specific circumstances dictate otherwise—you don't trust your executor completely—are often the way to go.

You will find other standard form provisions in a standard Will form, like a provision that revokes all prior Wills, and names the decedent's spouse and children. These should be left in, whenever appropriate.

The next thing you'll want to do is determine specific gifts: particular items that you want to go to particular people. This might be a set of golf clubs to your best friend, a house to your daughter, or money to your favorite charity. The only requirement is that you set it out particularly so that the item can be identified. Note that if you give a specific gift, other than a generic thing like money, and you no longer own that thing at your death, by law the gift will lapse, and the person will get nothing. If this is not what you want to happen, you can put in a provision that specifies an alternative, if the property is no longer owned by you at death.

Another way to give a specific gift, which many of our clients like to point out, is to forgive a debt owed to you. The $700 your cousin Fred owed you for ten years can be your gift to him—or to others; after all it is an asset of your estate.

Making specific gifts can be a major part of your Will or none at all, but either way, you need a "residuary clause"—a catch-all section that names the person or persons who get what is left (often called the "residuary beneficiary"). Why do you need this type of clause? Because even if you identified and gave away every specific item you own in your Will, there is always something left out, either because you forgot it or acquired it after you made the Will. A residuary clause covers those things.

Indeed, as suggested above, some Wills, in fact most, do not make specific gifts, or, if they do, they are a small part of the Will, because the bulk of the assets are left to the heirs through a residuary clause. The residuary clause is a neat, shorthand way to leave the assets of an estate without having to detail specific gifts to specific people.

What Property Can Be Transferred by a Will?

The simple answer to this is: all property in the estate. However, if you're an inquisitive type, you would ask, "What property is in the estate?" and the answer to this question is not as easy. Consider the following situation:

> **My brother just died and left me his entire estate. In his Will, he specifically included a house he owned in joint tenancy with his ex-wife. Apparently, they had forgotten to take it out of joint tenancy before he died, but I'm sure he didn't intend for her to get it. Since he made the Will leaving me the property after the divorce, do I get the property?**

No. Joint tenancy property, as we will discuss in more detail in Chapter 7, is not part of the decedent's estate. It transfers immediately and automatically on death to the surviving joint tenant. Therefore, his half interest in the property would go automatically to the ex-wife, no matter what his intent. If he wanted his part of the property to go to his sister, he should have severed the joint tenancy prior to death. More on this later.

Here's another one:

> **My father set up a trust with several pieces of land for my sisters and myself. The instructions were to distribute the trust assets to us after his death, but I was given a lesser share because of problems**

we had with each other several years ago. Just before his death, we made up and he changed his Will, giving me an equal share. But my sisters are now saying that the change doesn't affect the distribution in the trust. Is this true?

Yes, unfortunately it is. Like joint tenancy property, property held in a trust is not part of the estate. Thus, any attempt to change the trust distribution by making a change in the Will would have no effect. If the father really wanted to make this change, he should have amended the trust, not his Will.

Other examples of property that are not part of the decedent's estate, and so not transferable by Will, are life insurance proceeds payable to a beneficiary and pay-on-death bank accounts.

When Is It Necessary to Update or Change a Will?

Here is an all-too-common misunderstanding:

I had a Will made before my divorce that leaves everything to my ex-wife. I'm now planning on getting remarried and would like everything I have to go to my new wife if something ever happens to me. Do I need to alter the Will, or does the law do that automatically because of the divorce and remarriage?

The law may, but I wouldn't count on it. If it doesn't, the ex-wife might get everything—less any statutory rights of the new wife (see page 47).

A Will is really much more temporary than most people think. As you go through life your circumstances change, and what you own—and how much you own of it —changes. Consequently, a Will made before a divorce or any other change-of-life event probably needs to be altered to reflect that change.

Thus, a Will is not designed to be a permanent fixture in your special document drawer. It is only designed to handle the here and now, and it is made to be modified. You should consider changing your Will after having a baby, getting married, getting divorced, the death of a close family member, buying a major asset like a house, or just changing your mind, among other times. Most estate planning attorneys advise their clients to come in and do an examination of their Will, if not their entire estate plan, once a year to see if any change is necessary.

Sometimes, state law may aid in changing a Will as a result of something happening, but this is the exception rather than the rule, and I wouldn't depend on it.

How should this change be accomplished? You have two choices:

(1) you can tear up the old Will and write a new one, following all the formalities you did the first time; or

(2) you can prepare and sign a codicil. A codicil is an amendment to a Will that changes it in parts, and yet does not discharge it. The Will

stays in effect as to all terms except those modified.

The codicil option is rarely used, because in order to make it effective, you still have to comply with all the requirements for a new Will. Therefore, most attorneys recommend redoing the entire Will.

How Can You Disinherit Someone?

Disinheriting sounds like pretty serious business. Consider the following:

> **I just found out that my son has gotten into drugs and is hanging around with a group of criminals. I want to make sure that he doesn't get anything from me when I die. I couldn't stand him using my money to buy drugs.**

You probably know people in this kind of situation. Their son or daughter is up to no good, and, among other things, they want to divorce him or her from their Will. So what should they do? They simply say so in the Will document.

"To my son, Dave, I leave nothing."

You can explain your reasoning, if you want, or leave one dollar (it seems less harsh to say "I leave Dave one dollar"), as many attorneys advise, but these extras are not necessary. Just say it straight out and clear.

The reason you need to do this in the first place is because state law in many states provides for the assumption that if a child of a decedent is not mentioned in his or her Will, it was a mistake and he or she is entitled to take a share of the estate anyway. This is designed to protect children born after the Will was made, but may affect the situation described above, if the child is not specifically disinherited in the Will.

The problem of disinheritance can be a little more complicated in the case of a spouse. Many states provide for what is commonly referred to as a "forced share" or "elective share" of a spouse. A forced share is a statutory right of a spouse to collect a share (usually one third) of her husband's (or his wife's) estate, regardless of what is contained in the Will. For a listing of such states, see the chart on page 48.

If you are in one of these states, you may have to divorce your spouse to disinherit him or her—which may not be a bad idea, if things are so bad that you want to disinherit him or her. The only other possible way to disinherit is through a marital property agreement where the spouse waives all rights to an inheritance, but this is not effective in all states.

In states that allow disinheritance of spouses, you will have to specifically disinherit the spouse, as was discussed for children. Be sure in both cases, however, that you're comfortable with what you're doing. Disinheritance is a harsh thing to do to a close family member like a spouse or child, and can leave scars or may develop into a Will contest.

Consider other options, like restrictive gifts combined with no contest clauses, such as prohibiting access

**States Providing for
Some Form of a Forced Share**

Alabama	Iowa	New Hampshire	South Carolina
Alaska	Kansas	New Jersey	South Dakota
Arkansas	Kentucky	New York	Tennessee
Colorado	Maine	North Carolina	Utah
Connecticut	Maryland	North Dakota	Vermont
Delaware	Massachusetts	Ohio	Virginia
District of Columbia	Michigan	Oklahoma	West Virginia
Florida	Minnesota	Oregon	Wyoming
Georgia	Mississippi	Pennsylvania	
Hawaii	Missouri	Rhode Island	
Illinois	Montana		
Indiana	Nebraska		

to the inheritance until the child is certified as completing a drug rehabilitation program.

Note that, unlike a child or spouse, you don't have to specifically disinherit your other relatives. Your brother, mother, cousin, or aunt, for example, can be disinherited simply by not mentioning them in your Will, and giving the property to someone else. The law does not give them automatic rights, as it might for children and/or spouses.

What Kind of Limitations Can Be Put on Gifts Made in a Will?

If you think about it, when you make a "devise" (a gift) in a Will, what you're doing is making a gift after you die—a pretty amazing feat.

But for some people, and in some situations, this isn't enough—they need control.

What kind of control can be exercised after death? The kind that says how, when, and where a gift can be used, or how someone must behave in order to get the gift and keep it.

Here are a few samples:

To my cousin Bob, I leave my house and cash in the bank, on the condition that he take care of my aunt Martha and allow her to live with him for the remainder of her life.

To my son, Ray, I leave my special hunting rifle and $10,000 if he takes and finishes a three-month drug rehabilitation program.

To my loving wife, I leave the remainder of my estate for so long as she is alive, but when she dies, or if she ever remarries, then the property shall pass to my sister Millie.

This is dead hand control—an attempt by the dearly departed to control the use and enjoyment of property, or the people they give it to, after their death. I say attempt, because sometimes these restrictions are not successful for one of two reasons: the recipient of the gift refuses to comply, and so rejects the gift; or the restriction is not enforceable by law.

Whether or not a restriction is enforceable is controlled by state law and individual court sentiments as to public policy. If this sounds complicated, that's only because it is. In fact, I would not advise anyone to attempt the creation of restrictions on property use after death without, at least, getting them reviewed by an experienced estate planning attorney.

For those of you who insist on pushing on without help, here are a few general things to consider before attempting to place limitations on your estate gifts:

First, consider that you may be better off using a trust than a Will if after-death controls are a central part of your estate plan. A trust, as we shall see, allows you to take control of the property away from the beneficiary and put it in the hands of an independent trustee who you control by trust instructions. Being a trustee, he or she can be held liable if your instructions are not followed.

In either case, however, limitations on the use of a gift after death, especially if that gift is of real property, like land or a house, are subject to several legal challenges. These challenges, while different in title, involve the same underlying principle: restrictions on the use of a gift violate public policy by prohibiting the highest and best use of the property.

This singular concept gives judges the authority to void the restrictions and thus defeat the intent of the grantor of the gift. Maybe more importantly, however, it gives the recipient grounds to challenge the restriction.

Why more importantly? Because, as you are starting to learn, few things are absolute in the law. Inconsistencies and ambiguities in statutes and court decisions leave room for judicial interpretations, and individual judges have individual views of how things should be treated. This means that few decisions are a certainty, and most everything is a negotiation—if for nothing else, to save time and money. This is especially true in cases where the person who created the restriction is dead, and no one is around to defend his or her intent.

In short, deals are cut and restrictions taken off property by agreement of the surviving parties. Thus, if you want your restrictions followed, you'll have to set them up to bypass these rules and give someone an incentive to see that they're enforced. A discussion with a local attorney who understands the rules is the best way to make this happen, but if this option is not available, consider the following:

(1) *Limit the restriction as to time.* Restrictions that continue on and on, ad infinitum, are rarely enforceable. Indeed, the shorter the better, from the standpoint of enforcement. If Aunt Martha in the first example is ninety-two years old and in bad health, this restriction will not seem as onerous to Cousin Bob and will seem very reasonable to a court. She doesn't have long to live and probably needs the help. In any case, this restriction is limited to the length of Martha's life, and that alone may make it enforceable.

(2) *Make the restriction a condition precedent to*

getting the gift rather than a condition subsequent—a condition that would cause any interest to be lost if not met. This is not always possible, but if you can prohibit the person from getting the property until they have done what you want, you will be more likely to have it enforced than if the restriction tries to take the property away for failing to do something later. The situation in the second example above shows how this might be done; Ray is required to finish his rehabilitation program *before* he gets the money and the rifle.

(3) *Create an adverse interest: someone who has incentive to enforce the restriction.* This usually means a person who will take the property if the original recipient violates the limitation. This kind of backup enforcement is shown in the third example, where the sister, Millie, gets the property if the wife ever remarries.

What Can Be Done to Stop Will Contests?

A Will contest is a challenge by a beneficiary or person left out of a Will to the distribution as contained in the Will. The most obvious cause is a dissatisfied close relative or a person who was promised something by the decedent —people with an expectation of benefit that is not realized by the distribution made in the Will. Another cause is when there is reason to believe that someone has tampered with the Will, or exerted undue influence over the decedent. A key part of any estate plan involving a Will is to try to keep these situations from ever happening.

There are only a few grounds upon which a Will can be challenged. These are:

(1) the decedent was under age at the time the Will was made and was therefore unable to make a Will;

(2) the decedent was incompetent at the time the Will was made and was therefore unable to make a Will;

(3) the decedent was subject to an undue influence or the victim of fraud or duress at the time the Will was made; or

(4) the Will formalities (as discussed above) were not complied with.

The first and best defense against someone challenging your Will is to examine these factors and make sure you comply. Numbers one and four are the easiest, as your age is a foregone conclusion, and the formalities are easily complied with if you know what they are—as you now do. This is why almost all challenges are based on either the incompetence of the decedent or undue influence, fraud, or duress.

Competence to make a Will is generally based on the person's ability to understand the nature and extent of their estate (assets) and the distribution they are making through the Will at the time they sign it. If there is a question as to competence, as when the person is in a hospital or has been recently released, it may be a good idea to get a medical opinion as to the person's ability to understand what's going on, before signing the Will. It may also be a good idea to arrange for a videotaping of the decedent reading the Will. This can often be used as evidence if the decedent at least appears competent and not under any undue influence. It is important to note that there is generally a presumption of competence, meaning that the challenger has the burden to prove the decedent was incompetent.

Undue influence commonly involves pressure put on the decedent by someone who is in a "fiduciary relationship" with him or her. A fiduciary relationship is a special relationship beyond the normal arm's-length dealings we have with one another; one in which the decedent is in a dependent position, and thus needs to trust that the fiduciary will advise and treat him or her fairly and honestly.

A trustee of a trust obviously should have this relationship with the beneficiaries of the trust, and a doctor should have this relationship with his patients in regard to medical matters. A mother may have this relationship with her minor child, and anyone may have such a relationship with someone who is incapacitated and requires their care.

When someone in this position of control also turns out to be the main beneficiary of a Will—especially when this doesn't appear to be a natural result—the Will is ripe for a challenge.

A most obnoxious example of this sort of abuse of power involved the case of a California attorney whose clients, almost all elderly, seemed to always feel such gratitude for his services that they would leave him large sums of money, often to the exclusion of their own children and family. The family would on occasion—if they were alive —challenge the gifts, but of course, the cost of such a challenge against a local attorney would almost always lead to a settlement. The attorney was eventually stopped, but not until a *Los Angeles Times* news story brought his escapades to the public's attention and the state Bar Association finally took action.

On the other hand, persons often want to give a gift based on love, affection or gratitude—rather than undue influence—to someone in a fiduciary relationship with them. If this is the case, it's advisable to bring in the intervention of a third party to advise the person making the Will as to their rights. For example, no legitimate estate planning attorney would write a gift in a Will to themselves, or to anyone in their family, without first bringing in another attorney to advise the client and do the drafting. I would be suspicious of any attorney who suggests otherwise.

Fraud occurs in these situations when someone knowingly makes false statements of fact with the intent to persuade another to make a Will as suggested by the defrauding party. There are several elements in this statement, all of which must be proven to make a successful fraud challenge: a false statement or omission; knowledge of the falsity; intent; reasonable reliance; and damage.

As you might guess after seeing these requirements, fraud is an even tougher and less likely challenge than undue influence. It is also quite a bit more involved than many people think. Indeed, generally, most clients believe all they need to show to make a fraud challenge is that someone lied—not true, and not enough. It is not fraud, for example, in this sort of common complaint:

My aunt just died and my cousin was named in the Will to receive half of her estate. He is such a fraud, kissing up to the old lady in the last days of her life to get in good. I was closer and far nicer to her than he ever was, until the last few months. Can I challenge the Will based on this?

This is not the type of fraud that makes up a Will challenge. A true fraud for this purpose usually involves someone who has made a deal with the decedent under false pretenses, promising to do something with the money or property inherited, which he or she never intends to do. In other words, real Will fraud involves an elaborate plan created just to trick the decedent into putting the beneficiary in the Will.

The last defense, duress, is also commonly misunderstood. Most people seem to think that duress occurs when someone is pressured into doing something they wouldn't otherwise do. Surprise! Not so in the legal sense, unless the pressure is so high that it takes away the person's free will and they have no other choice. This leads to all sorts of possible bizarre scenarios of coercion, starting with the person signing a Will with a gun literally to his head—clearly duress—and moving to less coercive situations, such as when a person is merely threatened with violence at a later time if they don't draft a Will the way the other person wants. As the threat becomes less immediate (allows the decedent time to avoid it) or severe (does not involve death or great bodily harm to the person making the Will), the challenge of duress becomes less viable.

Of course, these kinds of nasty scenarios are extremely rare in a Will situation. Who would sign a Will with a gun to their head (the next thing would be for the gunman to shoot), and who would attempt to force someone to sign a Will like this without killing them immediately afterward? (Otherwise the Will maker could simply and secretly revoke the Will later by making another.) And, of course, there is always the fact that a murderer cannot inherit from his victim—at least in most states.

A criminal inclined to such violent threats would also not, I would think, be inclined to wait for the person to die naturally. They would just take what they wanted immediately, and not fool around with a Will.

This is why most Will contests are based on incompetency or some form of undue influence. Most of these contests are begun because someone in the family is unhappy with what they got, or didn't get, in the Will.

The best way to avoid this is to avoid the surprise. Gather the family around after making a Will and explain what you've done and why you did it, with all present. It's no guarantee against a challenge, but it may help.

How Does a "No Contest" Clause Work?

A no contest clause is a provision in a Will that penalizes a beneficiary who makes a challenge. It's usually phrased as follows:

> **If any beneficiary under this Will in any manner, directly or indirectly, contests or attacks this Will or any of its provisions, any share or interest in**

my estate given to that contesting beneficiary shall lapse. If any share or portion of such share so lapsing would, in the absence of this paragraph, pass by intestate succession to the contesting beneficiary, or to the issue of the contesting beneficiary, such share or portion thereof shall instead augment proportionally all other gifts provided for in this Will, other than specific, demonstrative, or general gifts.

The intent here is to scare away would-be challengers by putting them at risk of losing it all if their challenge fails. Something to make one think before acting.

Note that this clause does not constitute a guarantee against Will contests, any more than the suggestions made above do. Consider the following situation:

I have been named executor of my father's Will, which leaves me everything and nothing to my brother. Last week he called and said he intends to challenge the Will under the theory that Dad was incompetent, and wanted to know if I was willing to settle the matter before going to court. The Will contains a no contest clause. Doesn't this prohibit him from making this type of challenge?

No. And because the brother has nothing to lose, since the Will gave him nothing, the clause has no teeth in its threat of disinheritance.

For a no contest clause to work, it has to be applied against a person who gets something of enough value to make it too risky to challenge. Outside of this, the only costs to the challenger are legal fees, time, and aggravation, the same as in any other lawsuit. But unlike other lawsuits, the challenge is against a pot of money that no living person yet owns. The decedent is dead and the other beneficiaries don't yet have it in their hot little hands. Thus deals can be made, which is what many contestants depend on in order to get something from nothing in the Will.

CHAPTER FOUR

Trusts

―――

What Is a Trust?

A trust is simply a method of holding property whereby title is split between a trustee, who is said to hold "legal title," and a beneficiary or beneficiaries, who are said to have "equitable" title. The trustee has control over the use of the property, but is restricted in his exercise of this control by the terms of the declaration of trust (the trust agreement), and what is called his "fiduciary duties" to the beneficiaries. More on this on page 91.

There is nothing magical about a trust, but it does have what appear to be magical effects. Most importantly, because the property in the trust is no longer held in the name of a decedent, it is *not* treated as part of a decedent's estate for probate purposes. This, of course, means probate avoidance.

The topic of trusts starts to become confusing when descriptive words are used to designate the particular type of trust being created. You've probably heard terms like *living trust, revocable trust,* or even *revocable living trust,* and wondered what special qualities they had. Or how about a *life insurance trust,* a *generation-skipping trust,* a *Q-TIP trust,* a *marital trust,* an *A-B trust,* a *Totten trust,* a *real estate trust,* or an *inter vivos* ("between the living") *trust,* to name a few.

If you are up on this sort of stuff, you already understand that the word that precedes the word *trust* is only a descriptor of some factor that is incorporated into the trust—and there may be more than one. Thus, a living trust (also called an inter vivos trust) is simply a trust created by a living person. It may be revocable and thus be a revocable living trust, and it may contain real estate as its principal asset, and thus be a real estate trust. Note that even though it was still revocable and made by a living person, we can drop those descriptors in favor of the one that points out the factor we are most interested in at the time—which in this case was real estate.

We will discuss the other descriptors above and what their key factors involve later in the book. For now, the importance of this explanation is to remove the mystery and magic a trust may connote. Visions of a Kennedy or Rothschild trust—or any trust for the children of the superrich—can skew a person's perception, making them susceptible to the sales scams of persons offering to create living trusts for their family's benefit. The following is typical:

> **I've been working with an estate planner and we've set up a living trust. He informs me I won't have to pay any estate taxes or go through probate, and I like that, but I was wondering whether there's any way to avoid the hassle of transferring my property into the trust and paying the annual maintenance fees?**

This caller paid $1,750 to have the trust documents created, and then agreed to pay an annual maintenance fee for the trust's upkeep, apparently to save taxes and avoid probate. His irritation now is the continuing cost and hassle of maintaining the trust as a separate entity. A closer look at what a trust is would have told him immediately that maintaining the trust by ensuring assets are transferred into the trust name is a critical part of obtaining the trust benefits. Remember, all a trust is, is a form of ownership. If you don't transfer the property into that form, it's *not* in the trust.

Moreover, this caller apparently believes that the trust will provide him with tax benefits. In this regard, he either misunderstood the sales pitch or was lied to. There were no tax benefits gained from the trust he described. In fact, the tax benefits a trust can offer are very limited and available only in a few specific circumstances. This point is so widely misunderstood that it bears emphasis:

> **There are no *income* tax benefits to setting up a standard revocable trust, and to the extent that**

there are *estate* tax benefits, they are limited to only a few very specific circumstances and specially drawn trusts.

The statement by this caller that he would not have to pay any estate taxes was true, but not because of the trust. His estate (about $250,000) was too small to be taxed. The trust had no effect on this. Remember, all he did was change the form of ownership. No magic.

The $1,750 price tag for this trust wasn't bad, but it wasn't that great either. You can get a simple living trust done for a good bit less—or you could pay more, if you're the type that likes to pay high-end retail.

The real question, however, isn't the price he paid, but whether he got something he needed. He had a small estate at the time, which involved a house, a car, and a life insurance policy, and he was married with no children. He could have simply changed title in the house and car to joint tenancy, and put his life insurance in his wife's name. There were no tax implications to this estate, and these moves would have avoided probate without the cost and hassle of the trust.

I'm not saying this was the way to go, but it was an option—an option I'm sure his estate planner overlooked. A warning: Salespeople are salespeople, whether selling cars, real estate, or estate plans.

When Should You Set Up a Trust?

The question anyone thinking about setting up a trust should ask is: What am I trying to accomplish? This will not only help determine whether a trust makes sense, but what kind of trust should be set up if it does.

The primary reason most people set up a trust is to *avoid probate*. "I want to avoid probate," I'll hear a client say, and I'll want to test their resolve by asking, "Why?" But I know why, as you now do—it's to save the surviving family members the time, money, and hassle a probate process involves.

Still, it's important to remember this underlying reason, so that you will not create the same problems in the here and now just to avoid them after you've gone. A balance is what you're after, seeking a benefit proportionate to the cost. If avoiding the costs of probate is your only goal or the only benefit a trust offers, you must measure this against the cost and hassle of setting up and maintaining the trust, and consider any alternatives that might be available.

Thus, your formula for determining whether or not to set up a trust might be:

benefits of trust versus *costs of setup* compared to *alternatives*

I realize this is easier said than applied. For one thing, how do you quantify the benefits or even the costs; for another, on what basis do you compare alternatives?

It's all very subjective—based on your personal view of the world.

As inexact as this formula may seem, it's still the only true formula a person can use to determine whether or not to set up a trust. Consider the following:

(1) *Determine how much you will save.* Probate costs usually run from 5 to 8 percent of the gross value of the estate. Thus, if the estate is small, the benefits of avoiding probate are going to be small also. If other goals, like tax savings, can be obtained through special trusts, such as a marital or Q-TIP trust (to be discussed in Chapter 9), add the savings provided on the plus side of your balance sheet in favor of the trust.

(2) *Investigate the various ways of setting up a trust.* The cost of setting up a trust can vary from a few dollars to a few thousand dollars, depending on how you set it up and what you want to accomplish. Obviously, if you can save some dollars in setup, the trust is more likely to make sense in the cost/benefit analysis.

(3) *Investigate the different alternatives to a trust.* If you know your goal, and there are other cheaper, faster, easier, or even better ways to accomplish it than a trust, like setting up a joint tenancy for a house to avoid probate, you will want to consider them. On the other hand, as we shall see, often these alternatives will have costs or limitations of their own that should be taken into account.

Not surprisingly, and despite the formula, a trust in one form or another is often a good idea for any reasonably good-size estate. What *is* a reasonably good-size estate? This may sound lawyerly, but I don't have an exact answer, because it varies with each person.

Some planners say that everyone needs a trust. I don't agree. I would say that most people with net estates of over $600,000, especially if they are married and/or care about their family, can benefit from some form of trust. Still, there are reasons why people with estates above this magic figure may not want to bother with a trust, and reasons why people below it should.

I generally advise people with net estates below $100,000 to think twice before creating a trust. A partial list of specific situations for which a trust may *not* be a good idea include:

(1) People without many assets (for the reasons discussed above).

(2) When the assets are not currently owned, but are only expected to be acquired, such as through an inheritance, a pending sale, or an agreement of sale on property. Without ownership, the property cannot be transferred into the trust.

(3) When simpler means of transfer after death, such as joint tenancy or life insurance, are available.

(4) Young, healthy people unlikely to die. If in this case the first situation is also true, it may not be worth going through the trouble of setting up a trust and maintaining it.

What Can a Trust Do?

We have already seen many things that a trust can and can't do. It can avoid probate by taking assets out of your name and putting them into the name of the trust. When you die, there is no need to transfer property to your beneficiaries through a probate—it can go to them through the trust instructions. For example:

> **Harry Smith sets up a trust. We might call him the "settlor" or the "grantor" of the trust. He names himself trustee, and his wife and himself as the beneficiaries of the *income* interest on the trust property. He also names his wife as successor trustee (the person who takes over as trustee if he dies), and his kids as the beneficiaries of the trust after he and his wife die (the *remainder* interest). He then transfers his property into the trust, retaining the right as settlor to terminate the trust at any time, and the right as trustee to do anything he wants with the property.**

This is a basic revocable living trust.

What has changed in Harry's life? Nothing. He can still do anything he wants with the property—within the law—to the point of canceling the trust and taking it back. But what he's done from a legal standpoint is quite significant and effective for the purpose of avoiding probate. When he dies, the property in the trust stays in the trust. He can no longer act as the trustee, of course, because he's dead. His wife automatically takes his place as the successor trustee, and if she is unable or unwilling to take control, another person can be appointed to take her place.

The benefits of the property go exclusively to the wife until she dies, and then to the children. They can then continue on with the trust or terminate it, depending on the terms. A probate of Harry and his wife's estate has been bypassed, and their property has passed to their children without having to resort to a court process or pay court expenses.

This doesn't mean a trust guarantees no litigation. Battles over the right to trust property can be just as costly and nasty as battles over a probate estate. What, for example, would happen if the wife in the example decided to terminate the trust and take all the property for herself after Harry died? Would her own children sue her? What if they were children from Harry's previous marriage?

The second thing a trust *might* do is save estate taxes, though *not income taxes*. I say this with some trepidation, because so many callers misunderstand the tax benefits of a trust.

Take another look at the Harry Smith Trust. Harry really did nothing except change ownership from himself, individually, to a trust that he fully controlled and received benefits from until the day he died. People who believe they can do this *and* avoid tax liability must also believe in magic and the tooth fairy. Just by virtue of his maintaining control over the trust—any control—the assets of the trust become taxable as part of Harry's gross estate for estate tax purposes.

The Internal Revenue Code makes everything a decedent owns, controls, or has an interest in a part of his estate for purposes of calculating the tax. Thus, in order to make an asset nontaxable for estate tax purposes—get the asset out of the estate—a person would have to give up all ownership, control, and interest—a potentially dangerous and costly proposition—just to save a few dollars in taxes after death. Trusts that do this and other special tax tricks, like trusts that utilize the maximum uniform estate tax credit between married persons, will be discussed in Chapter 9, but for now it is enough to know that there is a price to pay for trusts like these, and they are generally not recommended or even available except in specific circumstances.

The last thing a trust can be used for is to manage property, or, as discussed in the chapter on Wills, restrict access and control over property by the beneficiary. This is commonly done for persons with disabilities, children, or others who cannot care for or manage property themselves. This usage makes sense when the settlor cannot or does not wish to manage the property directly—after death, for example.

How Does a Trust Affect Debts?

Generally, it doesn't, but this is another area where misinformation and confusion are all too common. The following question is typical:

I'm concerned about my liability for an accident I was in last month. It was my fault, and I'm afraid

**the people I hit are going to sue me for more than
my insurance coverage, which is minimal. I have
a house and several other assets that someone
told me I should put in a trust. Will this trust protect my assets from the claims of these and other
creditors if I'm sued?**

Anyone who attempts to sell you a trust as a protection against creditors, unless the trust is irrevocable, is
selling you a bunch of hot air. There is no law anywhere
that protects assets in a revocable living trust against the
claims of creditors of the settlor (or beneficiaries who
have current vested rights to trust benefits). A revocable
living trust is not a separate entity that protects assets
against the lawful claims of creditors. It's as simple as that.

If you want to go so far as to set up a bona fide
irrevocable trust—a trust that cannot be terminated or
controlled by the settlor and is set up for the benefit of
someone else—then you may be able to create something
that is impervious to creditor's attacks. However, even
then, the trust must be set up for *bona fide* purposes, not
related to, or with the intent of, defrauding creditors. It
cannot, therefore, be done just prior to the creditors
showing up on your doorstep demanding payment.

On the other hand, an interesting and not untypical
situation is when a trust is used to protect against creditors of a beneficiary, not a settlor. For example:

**I am a widower and have been diagnosed with ter-
minal cancer. I have two children, one of whom
has had a great amount of financial difficulties in
his life, and I am afraid that if I leave him any-**

thing, his creditors will take it or he'll run through it and nothing will be left for when he really needs it.

This situation calls for a "spendthrift trust"—a trust that limits a beneficiary's access to trust property by giving the trustee complete control and discretion over when to make a distribution of trust assets or income. If done correctly, this takes the trust assets out of the reach of the beneficiary and thus the beneficiary's creditors—at least until the trustee decides to make a distribution of trust assets.

How Do You Create a Trust?

Many people are concerned over the complexity of setting up a trust, but, to tell the truth, it's not really that difficult. In fact, there are only two parts to the creation of an active trust: the declaration of trust, and the transfer of property into the trust.

The declaration of trust is the document the settlor signs to create the trust relationship and terms. Samples of this type of document can be found in self-help books (for around $20) describing how to do it yourself. Attorneys and others, such as independent paralegals, offering trust services are also abundant, if you would rather have someone else do it for you (for $300 and up for a simple trust). The choice is yours, as are the terms.

In fact, one of the beauties of a trust is the flexibility

you have in deciding what you want in it. There is no one to negotiate with, as there is when you make a contract; you have total control. However, if you want certain special treatment of property in the trust, like spendthrift protection, you will need to take care in how you make these choices. We will discuss other kinds of special treatment later in the book.

While most people understand that they must put together the proper document to set up a trust, they often fail to realize they must also transfer their property into the trust name—the second part of the trust equation. Several years back, this happened to a friend of mine. He knew he was dying of cancer, and had substantial assets, so he carefully planned his estate using a trust. He hired a good estate planning attorney (not me—I was too close, and didn't want to get involved in the legal aspects), and had the trust instrument drafted and executed. The attorney gave him specific instructions on transferring his property into the trust, but, understandably, his mind was elsewhere and he didn't make all the transfers. In addition, he sold some of his property and bought others as the disease went into remission and then came back a few times. Eventually he got tired of the battle against the cancer and killed himself, without making the final transfers.

His daughter, his sole heir and beneficiary, called me a few months later frustrated and angry over the legal mess that was left. Some of his property was in the trust, some was not, and some she couldn't even find. The stuff that was not in the trust had to go through probate, making the declaration of trust, for all its wonderful legalese, a failure in achieving its purpose of avoiding probate, at least for those assets.

What Formalities Need to Be Observed in Making a Legal Trust?

The average person, I have found, imagines all sorts of magical incantations that must be performed in order to create a trust. It is thus often a surprise to find out how simple and few the formalities are. Basically, the declaration of trust need only provide for:

(1) the appointment of a trustee,
(2) the designation of a beneficiary,
(3) the dated signature of the settlor (preferably notarized so it can be recorded, if desired), and
(4) a certification that the document contains the correct terms of the trust.

A trust does not need to be recorded; nor does it need to be signed before two or three witnesses, as does a Will; nor does it need to be on special paper, approved by a court or county officer, or even produced by an attorney. Surprised?

One last point: You do not, as some people believe, need to set up a new trust if you move to a new state. Trusts are valid in all fifty states and so can move with you. You may, however, wish to consult counsel when you move as to possible changes in state law treatment of the trust property. For example, when you move to a community property state from a common-law state you may find that some of the property you thought was exclusively yours is now partly your spouse's by state law.

What Should Be in a Declaration of Trust?

There are several items that should be in a trust, some basic and some not so basic. The following is a general list.

1. *The Trust Name.*

You will need to name the trust. This is typically your own name followed by the word *trust* or *family trust* (for example, the Smith Family Trust), but this is not necessary. A trust can be named anything you like; the only purpose here is for identification.

2. *The Trustee.*

You will also need to name a trustee or cotrustees. Typically, the initial trustee of a living trust is the settlor (you, if you are setting up the trust), or the settlor and his or her spouse as cotrustees if it is a marital trust. This lets you remain in control of the property you transfer to the trust. You may, however, want to name someone other than yourself as initial trustee because you cannot or do not wish to manage your own property. If you do something unusual like this, I advise you to obtain expert help in devising the controls necessary to protect against trustee abuses.

Moreover, you should follow the designation of the initial trustee with the name of a successor trustee, a person who will take over the job when the original trustee or trustees die or are unable to continue as trust managers. You can also add an alternate successor trustee if the person or entity named as successor trustee is unavailable or unwilling to perform as trustee when called on to serve. Make sure your trust specifically reflects the circumstances upon which the successor trustee can take control —the death or incapacity of the original trustee.

You can name more than one trustee or successor trustee, but I generally do not recommend it outside of a marital trust. If there is more than one trustee at any time, the law requires they agree on all actions before proceeding. This, as you might expect, can often lead to coordination problems and conflicts. I have seen more than one brother-sister relationship deteriorate under this type of scenario, but, then again, I have also seen such relationships deteriorate when only one sibling is the trustee and the other doesn't like what he or she is doing. This may be reason enough to separate children by requiring an early distribution, creating separate trusts, or appointing an independent trustee.

It is also a good idea to avoid institutional trustees—banks, trust companies, and the like—when possible, as they tend to be less receptive to the needs of your family.

3. *The Trustee's Powers.*

Much of the trust document is taken up by what the trustee can and cannot do, commonly referred to as the trustee's powers. This is, of course, less important when you are the trustee of your own trust, and more important when a successor trustee takes over.

In a typical revocable living trust, a successor trustee is only intended to gather the trust property and distribute it to the named beneficiaries, much like an executor of a Will. The trust will usually state how and to whom the property in the trust is to be distributed, and declare what decision-making authority the trustee will have in the process.

On occasion, however, more is required of the trustee—an obligation of management continuing for more than a short, interim period. When this is the case, you will want to be even more particular about the authority you give to the trustee or successor trustee. Which powers a trustee has is almost completely in your control, and you can usually pick from several variations in sample trust documents contained in do-it-yourself books.

While it is most important to consider a trustee's powers when dealing with a long-term trust, that is no reason to be lax in restricting a trustee who is given only short-term obligations. The following typical question indicates why:

My husband died several months ago, leaving two living trusts, one in which I am trustee and a second containing his business in which his partner, Bob, became the trustee of his interest after he

> died. The kids and I are the beneficiaries under
> both trusts.
>
> I know he felt that Bob would be the best
> person for the job, but he also expected that Bob
> would buy us out in a short period of time. In-
> stead Bob has continued to run the trust and
> elected to reinvest much of the money back into
> the business. We have been getting only a small
> part of the money made. He says he has the gen-
> eral power to do this under the trust in order to
> maintain the business, but I don't trust him any-
> more and would like to know what I can do about
> it.

This situation brings up several issues, not the least
of which is the importance of choosing a trustee carefully.
More than just someone who is competent and trustwor-
thy, you want someone who will sympathize with the
needs of the beneficiaries and not have a conflict of interest.

The husband in this situation left standard form general powers in his second trust, which gave Bob some
discretion as to what to do with the business income. As
long as he stayed within these powers and didn't waste the
trust assets—in fact, he was reinvesting in them—he
could not be charged with doing anything wrong. Of
course, our caller had other needs, and thus saw it differently. What do you think her dead husband would have
wanted? If not what his partner was doing, then he should
have arranged to limit these powers in the trust document.

As we shall discuss later, there are things that this

questioner can do to terminate the trust and get a final distribution, but such things would require legal action—without the cooperation of the trustee—and probably not give rise to any claim against the trustee for wrongdoing (unless more is going on here, like he has been taking trust property for his own personal use). Note the irony in that this is precisely what the trust was set up to avoid—court action and costs (probate).

A list of items to consider in choosing a trustee include:

(a) Should he or she post a bond as security for honest and faithful service? How much do you know and trust the person or entity who will be acting as trustee? Do you want some protection against dishonesty or malfeasance?

(b) Should he or she be paid any compensation? Usually this occurs only when the job entails some sort of ongoing management functions beyond the typical distribution of assets to the beneficiaries.

(c) Should he or she have the power to appoint successor trustees, or would you like to name them in advance yourself?

(d) Should he or she have the power to buy, sell, use, or encumber trust property, or borrow money, and to what extent?

(e) Should he or she have the power to continue to run a trust business? For how long, and under what circumstances?

(f) What special powers will the trustee need to do special tasks required by the trust?

Finally, a trustee often files the federal and state estate and death tax returns, and pays the tax, unless this is done by the executor of the Will (typically the same person). Thus, in most trusts, this should also be included as part of a trustee's powers.

4. The Beneficiaries.

A trust must also name a beneficiary or beneficiaries of the trust property. These are the people who are to receive the benefit of the trust property.

As with a Will, there can be beneficiaries who get specific property, called direct beneficiaries, and those that will get all trust property not specifically designated, called residuary beneficiaries. You can also name alternate beneficiaries, in the case that a specified beneficiary is unable to take his or her share (for example, if they die first).

Finally, if you plan to place limits on a specific gift given to a beneficiary, you should do it in the same part of the trust where you name the beneficiary and the property given.

5. The Trust Property.

The trust should contain a listing of trust property, usually attached as an exhibit or schedule to the declaration of trust. This is nothing more than the last page of the trust document, set aside as a list. The reason it is maintained separately is so you can update it from time to time to reflect new assets purchased and old assets sold. Remember that if something isn't listed and/or transferred into the trust, it may not be considered part of the trust, and so will fall under the Will—or if no Will, the intestate estate—and have to be probated.

The list should be as complete as possible at the time the trust is created, containing all assets you wish included in the trust, and then updated on a regular basis. A discussion of how property is transferred into the trust can be found on page 83.

6. Debts.

Taking care of lifetime debts is a necessary part of a trust. Some people are under the mistaken impression that a trust is impervious to the claims of creditors in life and after death.

"How can they find it?" I often hear people ask. "And if they find it, how can they get it when it's not in my name, it's in the name of the trust?"

The answer is that *they can*. So you might as well prepare yourself.

Generally, the successor trustee of a revocable living trust pays the decedent's bills after his or her death, or transfers the trust property subject to the debt to the appropriate beneficiary. You may want to make a provision specifically directing how debts are to be paid; otherwise, *any* property can be taken by the trustee to satisfy a debt, and this might be something you wanted to go to someone in particular.

With regard to debts that are tied to specific property

(secured debt), like a mortgage is to a house: there is no need to pay them off at death, unless you want to for some reason. They can go to the particular beneficiary or beneficiaries along with the property.

However, unsecured debts, like most credit cards, personal bank loans, taxes (income and estate), funeral expenses, and hospital expenses (last illness), generally must be paid off upon the death of the settlor. Most estates have only a small amount of such debt, and what exists can be paid off by life insurance proceeds or from the gift to the residuary beneficiary. If this is the case, you will not need to plan much for the payment of debts.

Still, you will find that most standard trust documents contain provisions that allow you to designate which property will be used to settle which debts, just in case you want to specify something other than the residuary estate. Liquid assets, those assets that can be easily turned into cash—like bank accounts, CD's, and the like —are typically better for the payment of debt, since they do not require a sale that may result in a loss of value. Note that it is not unusual for an asset to lose as much as 50 percent of its estimated value in a forced estate sale to cover debts. Note also that this may result in broader problems, such as the following:

> **I was given about $25,000 in a bank account held by my aunt Martha's trust, but the trustee used this money to pay off her hospital and funeral expenses and I ended up with only a few hundred dollars. Do I have any recourse?**

If the trust allowed this, no. The question is, did Aunt Martha intend this to happen? When specific property is designated to pay debt and is also left to a specific person, there is always the risk that it will not be available when the time for distribution comes. In legal terms, it is said to have lapsed.

How Does Property Get Transferred into a Trust?

Transferring property into and out of a trust is generally a simple process—after all, it's your property. For this purpose, you can divide property into two types: those that are "of record," or have documents of title (ownership), and those that are not.

Property not of record includes things like furniture, clothing, electronic equipment, and other items you have around the house. These are things that have no formal document of title showing ownership—nothing recorded with some official government or private entity. For this type of property the transferring process is simple: all you need do is list the property in the trust declaration, usually on a trust schedule contained at the end.

Later, when you buy new property that is not listed, you can just add it to the schedule, or type out a simple bill of sale (forms are available in most stationery stores) transferring ownership to the trust.

If you decide to sell property held in the trust, remember to sign as trustee—assuming you are the trustee;

if not, you should not be selling the asset—and take the item off the list of trust assets.

Property of record, on the other hand, must be more formally transferred into the trust through the official registrar of the property. Without this, the trust doesn't own the property, and—guess what?—the property must go through probate if you die. Property of record includes real estate; bank accounts (all kinds); stocks, bonds, and other securities; and almost all moving vehicles (cars, boats, planes). Anything, in short, that is registered or on record somewhere.

What do you need to do to transfer this type of property into a trust? Reregister it in the name of the trust. Here's what needs to be done for specific kinds of property:

1. *Real Estate.*

For all types of real estate (house, condominium, raw land) you need to prepare a deed transferring the property into the name of the trust. If you are married and jointly own the property with your spouse, then both of you should make the transfer. The easiest form of deed for this purpose is a quitclaim deed—a deed that does not contain any warranties of title, that is, guarantee of ownership. You can use a standard grant deed, which provides these warranties, but since you are transferring property from yourself to your trust, it's simply not necessary.

A quitclaim deed form can be found in most stationery stores, and there are several self-help books that can help you fill it out if you have any problems. They are extremely simple to complete. The most important thing to remember is to use the exact wording of the property description and the spelling of your name as contained in the original deed you received when the property was transferred to you. Then sign, notarize, and record the deed with the county recorder's office for the county where the property is located, and you will have fully transferred the property into the name of the trust.

For those of you who are concerned, a transfer of real estate into a revocable living trust does not have any underlying tax implications or effect on property rights (other than what may be required in the trust). This means that barring a special state law, there is no property tax increase, no loss of homestead rights, and no loss of federal tax benefits (such as the right to defer gain upon repurchase of a principal residence, and the $125,000 exclusion of gain for people over fifty-five) when property is transferred into a trust. *law changed in Aug 17*

2. *Bank Accounts.*

These are even easier than real estate, because your bank has the forms and your account representative can help you fill them out. As long as the bank recognizes the trust as owner of the account, you have done your job. Note there are certain types of accounts, such as a normal checking account, that you may not want to put into the trust. In such a case, you can make the account "pay on death" to the trust by arranging with the bank to name the trust as account beneficiary. By doing so you can bypass probate without having to include the account in the trust during your life.

3. Stocks, Bonds, and Other Securities.

These assets are also easily transferred, because the form and procedure is supplied by the company or government agency that issued it. Whether you own a mutual fund, a limited partnership interest, a U.S. T-bill, or stock in IBM, your first step is to call the issuing company, general partner, or agency and get their form for transfer. A good stockbroker will do this for you and fill out the forms when they come in. The company may require a copy of the trust with a letter instructing them to reregister the security in its name, and you may need to turn over the old stock or ownership certificates, if they are in your possession. Note, however, that if you can't find the certificates, there are always procedures for reissuance.

If you own your own corporation, or are actively involved in a relatively small general partnership, you'll probably need to have the stock certificates or partnership rights reissued into the name of the trust yourself. This simply involves getting the approval of any co-owners and making the change in the corporate books or partnership records. Remember that any such change will need to comply with the corporate bylaws or the terms of the partnership agreement.

Sole proprietorship businesses—businesses owned and operated by one person, which have not been incorporated—are not of record, and therefore only need to be listed in the declaration of trust. However, property that such a business owns, like real estate, should be transferred as outlined in that section.

4. *Vehicles.*

As you probably know, these are registered with the state, usually with an agency called the Department of Motor Vehicles. They provide the form and instructions—all you need to do is fill them out and stand in line. Check with your insurance agent, however, to make sure that your coverage will continue if title is changed. You may also need the permission of any banker or lender who has a lien on the vehicle.

Other vehicles, such as trucks, boats, and planes, may have federal agency registrations. If you own such an asset, you will need to contact the appropriate agency to make the transfer.

5. *Insurance, IRA's, and Other Assets That Can Name Beneficiaries.*

You do not need to reregister these kinds of assets into the name of the trust, even though they may be of record. All you need to do is name the trust as beneficiary, and the proceeds will go automatically into the trust, bypassing probate, when you die.

This is not a complete list, but you get the message. Any property that you own and want to be part of the trust must be listed in the trust document and/or registered in the trust name. If you fail to properly transfer property into the trust (even though you set it up), it passes outside the trust by Will, if you have one, to your residuary beneficiary, or to your next of kin under state intestate succession laws as discussed in Chapter 3. In addition to requiring probate, note that these may not be the people you intended to get this property. Therefore, be careful to make the proper transfers.

I have said before that this is all a simple process, and indeed it is, in a relative sense. It is simple enough to list items or to make the changes described in this section if you take the time. However, most people are not used to doing this in their day-to-day lives. Keeping track of assets and making sure they are included as part of the trust is often considered a hassle.

"I don't have time for this," I will hear a client say. "What a pain in the behind."

I mention this fact because it appears to be a real problem, about which many attorneys and estate planners do not advise their clients. You really need to be a type A personality (like an estate planner or attorney) to find this sort of tracking and maintenance no problem—unless, of course, you have no property (but then you don't need a trust) or you have enough money to have someone else handle the tracking for you.

Is the Transfer of Property into a Trust Subject to Gift Tax?

This will depend on the type of trust and how much the property is worth. Generally, however, a revocable living trust is not considered a completed gift, and therefore is not subject to gift tax, because the settlor can take the property back any time before death.

In addition, gifts under $10,000 in any given year are excluded from estate and gift tax. Further discussion of the tax implications of setting up a trust are contained in Chapter 9.

What Responsibility Does a Trustee or Beneficiary Have for the Debts of the Settlor-Decedent?

This question brings us to a very common concern and misunderstanding regarding estate and trust debts. The following illustrates:

> **My father died last month, leaving a living trust with several assets, including his house, a car, and a small bank account. I am named as trustee and a beneficiary with my sister. The problem is that the debts against his house and car, and other personal debts, exceed the value of these assets. He was seriously ill the last few years of his life,**

and ran up a lot on his credit cards, as well as hospital bills that exceeded his insurance coverage. As trustee and beneficiary am I liable for these? What should I do?

Neither the named trustee nor the beneficiary of the trust is personally liable for the settlor-decedent's debts. If our questioner here decided to walk away, refusing to act as trustee, creditors of his father's would not be able to hold him personally liable on these debts. This is the same as in the case of an executor or beneficiary under a Will, or the next of kin if there is no Will. Debts simply do not transfer automatically from a decedent to the representative or beneficiaries of his estate.

That is not to say the assets in the estate are free of creditors' claims just because they're given to a beneficiary; nor does it mean that a beneficiary cannot voluntarily agree to cover estate or trust debts in order to receive an asset or assets in the estate. This is, in fact, a common occurrence when the value of the assets exceeds the debts. The recipient of a house, for example, will often agree to take responsibility for an existing mortgage in order to keep the house.

Moreover, this is also not to say that a trustee of a trust, or executor of a Will, cannot do something in violation of a creditor's rights and so create personal liability for his or her acts; for example, distributing trust assets while ignoring the bona fide claims of creditors.

This is something for a trustee to think about before accepting the position, and for a beneficiary to think about before accepting a gift that is burdened with a debt. They have, after all, a choice in the matter.

What Are a Trustee's Duties to the Trust?

A trustee has, what is called in the law, a "fiduciary duty" to the trust and its beneficiaries. This means that a trustee must protect, watch, and maintain the trust property as he would if it were his own. Fiduciary duties also prohibit a trustee from making a profit as against the trust, using trust property for personal benefit, and other such things.

These fiduciary duties become most important when the trustee is an independent party attempting to administer the trust for the benefit of others. Take, for example, the following situation:

> **I am a beneficiary of a trust with my sister and she is also the trustee. She wants to sell our mother's home, which I think is a mistake in this bad market, and I believe she has already taken for herself two bank accounts that should have been shared with me under the terms of the trust. What are my rights?**

This is a classic problem. One sibling takes control of the estate and the other becomes suspicious. The one that is outside may just be paranoid or jealous, or may be rightfully concerned about abuses.

The remedy is an accounting.

In addition to his or her other duties, a trustee is required to account to the beneficiaries on a regular basis as to the state of trust assets—where they are, how much they are worth, and the like. If the sister has actually taken trust assets, it will show up in the accounting, unless, of course, she falsifies this report. If she does so or the accounting shows a mishandling of trust assets, the remedy is a court action for removal of the trustee for breach of her fiduciary duties. She will also be liable for the return of the assets wrongfully taken.

As to the determination of whether the house should be sold, this is usually within the sound discretion of the trustee and so would not create a cause of action against the sister, unless clear harm to the trust could be shown. It's important in these situations to investigate the trust document first, before taking any action, to compare what's been done to the powers given the trustee.

In any case, the first thing to do is to confront the trustee with your concerns, get an accounting, and try to work out a fair solution to the dispute. As always, a legal battle is an expensive way to solve a problem, and can have a serious negative impact on the continuing relationship of the parties—especially family members.

Finally, it should be remembered that a trustee has administrative duties to the trust operation. These include maintaining separate books and records, and filing informational income tax returns. This, however, is not required when the settlor is alive and acting as trustee of a revocable living trust.

What Special Concerns Exist in Trusts Set Up to Manage Property?

Interestingly enough, the trust mechanism was not originally designed as a probate avoidance device or even for the purpose of tax avoidance. In the beginning, the primary purpose of a trust was the management of property for those people or entities that needed an independent and/or centralized source of management. This is why a trust is designed with a separation of ownership between the trustee and the beneficiaries.

It should therefore be no surprise that several of the most frequently asked questions regarding trusts do not involve probate avoidance motives—at least not primarily —but address issues regarding the control or establishment of a trust to manage property. The following is illustrative:

I would like to establish an independent trust for my children in which their education is paid for out of the trust. Is there anything special I need to do?

Whenever a trust is established for a management purpose, there is the all-important issue of direction. The issue is a small one if the settlor is alive and acting as trustee. If a problem arises, he can resolve it without concern about whether his decision is in conformity with the purpose of the trust. As the settlor, he created the purpose; his intent controls.

But what happens when the settlor isn't around to

make the decision? Will an independent trustee make the correct choice—the one the settlor would have wanted—when a problem arises? The best way to assure this is to appoint a trustee who thinks like you and then give him specific instructions to follow.

Of course, a settlor can't think of everything. What if the questioner set up the educational trust and then died, leaving a friend to administer the trust for his children? Will the friend allow the trust to cover the cost of taking auto-mechanic courses? Graduate school? He will if the trust says so, and won't if it says not to. But if it says nothing, then the decision will be up to the trustee's discretion.

So the above questioner would have to establish what kind of education he or she was concerned about. Is it only for college, or also for graduate school? Does it include community colleges, or only universities? What about trade schools? Will he or she want the children attending full-time, or will part-time be acceptable? Does the trust include coverage for books as well as tuition? How about housing expenses during school?

There are other questions as well, such as will the payments between the children be equal, and what happens to the trust funds if one or more of the children don't go to school or money is left over after their education is complete? These and numerous other issues need to be considered and addressed in drafting ongoing trusts of this type, simply because the settlor won't be around, or won't have the power, to make them when they have to be decided.

For this reason, you may want to consider seeking the help of a specialist in these sorts of trusts before setting one up. A person such as this should have the experience to know the questions to ask—not the answers; you have those—so that your desires will be followed when the time comes.

There are several situations when a trust of this type can make sense. The following is a short list:

(1) When an incompetent party is involved. Someone who is under age, or mentally incapable of taking care of their own affairs.

(2) When there are too many beneficiaries to manage the property together, and you don't want the asset sold, at least for a while.

(3) When you are dealing with a person who you feel has a history of irresponsibility, such as people with drug or gambling problems, or a person whom you consider a spendthrift.

What Is a Bank Account Trust?

Actually, this question comes in different forms depending on what the caller has heard the trust account called. Sometimes it is referred to as a "pay-on-death account," sometimes a "bank trust account" and sometimes a "Totten trust," among others.

In each case it's simply a bank account in which there is a designated beneficiary in the event the depositor dies. It generally looks something like this: Michael A. Cane, ITF Susan Cane. The ITF stands for "in trust for."

This kind of account creates no rights for the beneficiary in the account, and therefore is quite different from a joint bank account, as shall be explained. It allows the depositor full control while alive, yet avoids probate and permits a specified person to directly receive the money when the depositor dies—if it's not withdrawn first.

Note, however, that if the beneficiary dies before the depositor does, and his or her name is not removed from the account, when the depositor dies the proceeds in the account will be distributed to the beneficiary's estate and go as directed by his or her Will—or by intestate succession if there is no Will.

What Must Be Done to Amend or Terminate a Trust?

If a trust is revocable, as most living trusts are, then the settlor generally retains the power to alter, amend, or terminate the trust at his discretion. A trust is altered or terminated simply by preparing a document with the intended changes or a statement of the settlor's intent to terminate. When you terminate a trust, you must also transfer any property in the trust out (the same way you transferred it in).

One of the nice things about a trust is its flexibility. As the settlor, you can add a new beneficiary, delete an old one, change a successor trustee, or alter the trustee's powers. You can also take some of the assets out of the trust, leaving the trust intact, if that suits your changed goals.

Changes of this type are made on a separate document called an "amendment to trust," rather than on the original trust document, in order to avoid later disputes regarding the changes made. Disgruntled beneficiaries have been known to challenge changes made to documents directly, claiming that the original version was improperly tampered with.

Remember it's not necessary to formally amend a trust to add property. All that is needed is to add the asset to the property schedule and transfer its title as discussed above. Make sure, however, that you have stated the proper distribution of this added property in the trust itself so that the correct person will receive it.

Revocation or amendment of a trust is not so simple after the settlor's death. At that point all the parties, trustees, and beneficiaries need to agree on any alteration or revocation that is contrary to the trust terms, or a court has to be convinced that changed circumstances have made the alteration or termination the proper solution. Consider the following example of this problem:

> **I am one of seven beneficiaries of a trust that contains a large ranch. The ranch has not been doing very well from an income standpoint, but it could be sold off to developers for a nice profit and the proceeds distributed among the beneficiaries. One of my cousins, who is also the trustee and the person who runs the ranch, disagrees and refuses to sell. He claims that it's just in a slump, and we would lose value by selling it now. This is fine for**

him—he gets paid for his work and has enough money to wait, but I need the money now. What can I do?

This is another classic conflict between the ones in control and the ones not in control of trust property. The ones not in control invariably want to terminate the trust and get what they can immediately. The ones in control generally want to continue the trust because of some future anticipated value increase.

Both views often have merit; the parties just have different priorities. How are they resolved? Like any other dispute, the parties either come to an agreement—a settlement—or they go to court and fight it out.

Before taking such a harsh step, however, it's always wise to consider the strength of your position measured by the terms of the trust and applicable law. In the case above, I would first ask whether the trust provided for a specific termination date, whether there were any provisions regarding voting for termination by beneficiaries or restricting the continuation of the ranch if it wasn't profitable, and what type of conflicts of interest does the trustee cousin have with the other beneficiaries?

On the other side of this inquiry I would ask if the trustee was given wide discretion on the issues of whether or not to terminate and how to apply proceeds, as is often the case. The answer to these questions will indicate how a court would likely decide the dispute, and so whether the questioner should pursue his challenge of his cousin into the court system.

Can an Irrevocable Trust Be Revoked?

Here is the horror story behind this question:

> **I set up an irrevocable trust for my son in which he gets $5,000 per month for life. I did it largely to get the assets out of my estate for tax purposes on the advice of my tax adviser. Except now my son never comes to see me, and I've heard from my daughter, his sister, that he spends the money on drugs. I don't need the money, but I want this stopped. How can I cut him off from the money flow?**

If the irrevocable trust was set up right, she probably can't stop the money flow, at least without his agreement. That's why they call them irrevocable trusts—because they're irrevocable. The person who creates an irrevocable trust gives up control over it. Obviously, anyone thinking about creating one of these trusts should consider the long-term consequences.

Having said this, one possible solution, outside of estate planning, is to get the boy declared incompetent because of his drug problem. If she can do this and get herself or someone else appointed conservator or guardian of his estate, at least he won't be able to use the money on drugs anymore.

CHAPTER FIVE

Disability and the Durable Power of Attorney

—

And now, as they say, for something completely different. Well, at least, different in the sense that you will be planning not for after death, but for disability.

And why not? If you can expend energy planning for a time after which you no longer need money, why shouldn't you expend energy planning for a time when you can really use it?

Consider this:

You are walking along one day enjoying a glowing sunset as it makes its way behind an office building, when an uninsured, drunk driver jumps the sidewalk and knocks you into the display window of a

local butcher shop. He goes to jail, but you are
unable to work, maybe forever. After getting out of
the hospital, you find yourself often confused and
bound to a wheelchair. It can happen to anyone,
without prior notice.

At this point, you need two things: someone to help
make your financial and health decisions, and a form of
income for support.

Whether you were hit by a car or a bus, or just
started to deteriorate from old age or disease, these are
the things you need to consider, and there are several
options:

(1) Trusts
(2) Durable Power of Attorney
(3) Disability Insurance
(4) Social Security Insurance
(5) Living Will

How Can a Living Trust
Help Plan for Disability?

As mentioned in the previous chapter, a living trust is a
very flexible instrument. In its basic form it allows for a
transfer of property into the control of an independent
trustee, who then manages the property for the benefit of
a beneficiary or beneficiaries. This instrument can thus be

used to achieve at least part of the disability planning goal: entrusting someone with financial decision-making power.

Of course, you will need to create a trust with a provision that either has an independent trustee from the beginning, or activates him or her if you become disabled. Most people choose a trust that does the latter, as they want to maintain control over their assets until disability or death.

While such a trust may help in planning for disability, it is not a complete solution, as seen from the following caller:

> **I was named as the successor trustee of a living trust my father set up a few years back. Recently he had a stroke, and I've been trying to take care of his affairs, but have run into a couple of snags. One is that he has received several checks that are not made out to the trust, but to him personally, and I wonder if I can cash them. Another is that I want to put Dad in a private health care facility, but my brother, who is one of the beneficiaries, wants to bring him home. Don't I, as the trustee, have the right to make that decision?**

Remember, a trustee has control only over property in the trust. Property that is outside the trust, and decisions regarding it, are outside her authority. This means that the questioner, as trustee, does not have the right to cash the checks made out to her father personally, and is not necessarily the one entitled to make his health care decisions. Indeed, by cashing the checks, she may be liable to other estate beneficiaries for "converting" or taking the property.

Thus, there are two limitations on using a trust exclusively for disability planning (besides the fact that it is a relatively expensive document if used just for this purpose): it gives authority to make financial decisions only for property in the trust and not for property left out of the trust or acquired personally after the disability took place; and it does not create any right or power to make health decisions on behalf of the disabled person.

In short, you need more than a general living trust in your disability plan.

What Is a Power of Attorney?

There seems to be a lot of mystery and confusion surrounding the power of attorney, which I attribute largely to the name. It sounds so . . . well, powerful: power, attorney. If I had a dime for every time someone called me with the following type of confused question, I bet I would have enough for a nice cruise around the Mediterranean:

> **My mother recently sued a contractor who took her money and didn't do the work. Because she was ill, I went to court on her behalf with a power of attorney she gave me, but the judge wouldn't let me talk and dismissed the case. How can he do this?**

A power of attorney is not the power to act as someone's attorney. It does not authorize you or anyone else without a license to practice law, to represent someone in court, or to provide them with any sort of legal services. In fact, there are laws regarding the unauthorized practice of law (UPL statutes) that subject people who attempt to act as lawyers, without a license, to potentially stiff penalties.

That is not to say the woman in the question above would be prosecuted for her innocent attempt at helping her mother. The UPL laws are generally applied to more serious and regular violations. But as she found, she could not handle the court action, which led to her mother's case being dismissed by default, because there was no one in court who could legally prosecute the case.

What, then, does a power of attorney do?

It gives a designated person, called the agent, holder, or attorney-in-fact, the ability to sign and make decisions on behalf of the person who signs, called the principal.

Obviously, before giving someone such power over your affairs, you want to make sure you fully trust them and that the power is appropriately limited so they don't go wild and sell you out to the highest bidder. Thus, if you wanted to give a power of attorney to a friend or family member to transfer a parcel of land you own, or to access your safety-deposit box at the bank while you were out of the country, you could give them a power of attorney that was limited to just those acts.

One shortcoming, or advantage, of a power of attorney—depending on how you look at it—is that it becomes invalid upon the death or disability of the principal. This means you cannot do what this person would like to do:

> I have a power of attorney for my aunt who died
> yesterday. Just before she died she told me to go
> to her bank and clean out her accounts, but I was
> so involved in taking care of her that I didn't get a
> chance to do so until now. Is there any problem
> with me taking the money out of her accounts to-
> day? I was hoping to avoid the probate process by
> doing so.

The problem is that the power of attorney she got from her aunt while the aunt was alive is no longer valid now that she is dead. She may be able to go to the bank and clean out the accounts, as long as the bank is unaware of the death, but if she does so, she will be wrongfully taking the money and subject to the claims of other beneficiaries.

Of course, if no one complains, the violation might go unnoticed, but that doesn't take away from the basic point: a power of attorney is only good while the principal is alive.

Another problem for people putting together a power of attorney is bad timing, as shown in the following situation:

> My father has not been doing well lately. He has
> Alzheimer's disease and has reached a point
> where he can't take care of himself anymore. I'm
> having him sign a power of attorney and bringing
> him to live with me, but my sister is already com-
> plaining that I will take advantage of him and
> wants him to live with her. If I get the power of

attorney signed first, will I be able to get her off my back?

Not necessarily, unless she voluntarily decides to back off. To make a valid power of attorney—or any legal document for that matter—the principal must be competent *at the time* he or she signs. This means the principal must be capable of understanding the nature and extent of the document being signed at the time they sign it.

Thus, if the Alzheimer's disease has deteriorated the father in the example above to a point where he isn't able to care for himself, he may not be competent enough to sign. If he signs anyway, the document may be challenged by the sister and held invalid by a court of law.

In any case, note that this would have to be a "durable" power of attorney to survive the disability, as shown in the next section.

What Is a Durable Power of Attorney?

A durable power of attorney, sometimes called a "springing" power of attorney, continues to be valid even after incapacity or disability.

How can this be done, following the rules stated in the last section?

The power must be created before the incapacity occurs, *while the principal is still competent,* not after. To make it something more than a traditional power, it is designed to be effective, or spring up, only upon incapacity. When properly established, it continues to be effective until either the principal dies or becomes competent again and revokes it, or a court overrides the power with an order appointing a conservator or guardian.

There are two types of durable powers of attorney: a financial power and a health care power. These powers can be combined into one document, or separated into two distinct instruments depending on your needs and the law of the state where you live.

A financial power of attorney is designed to give the attorney-in-fact management authority over the principal's financial affairs, such as the authority to make deposits and withdrawals from the principal's bank accounts, run the principal's business, or manage, buy, or sell the principal's investment portfolio.

A health care power of attorney is designed to authorize the attorney-in-fact to make medical and health decisions for the principal. This might include deciding on a method of treatment, the particular doctor or health care facility the principal will use, or whether to maintain life-sustaining procedures when the principal is terminally ill.

In the case of either a financial or health care power of attorney, the principal can generally make whatever limitations he or she wants. Note again, however, two important things that are true no matter what else is involved in putting together your durable power of attorney:

(1) it must be signed by a person while he or she is competent to do so;

(2) it is valid only as long as the person is alive, albeit disabled.

What Can a Durable Power of Attorney Do in an Estate Plan?

A durable power of attorney allows you to appoint someone to make your financial and health decisions if you later become disabled. The key value of the durable power of attorney is that it's made while you're competent, but is only effective after you become incompetent. This is the "springing" element of the power.

A regular power of attorney becomes effective immediately, creating the risk that the attorney-in-fact may use the power before you become incompetent. In addition, a regular power may not survive the disability, meaning that it would become invalid when you really needed it.

"But," you might say, "wouldn't all this just happen automatically, if I became incompetent? Someone would step in and take control of my finances and make health decisions, and that would be that."

Most likely, but who? Would it be the person you want? And how long would it take for that person to be appointed by a court? Would there be a dispute between more than one person for the position? Wouldn't you like to have some say in the matter?

If you don't care, or have a virtual certainty as to who it would be, think again before dismissing the problem. What if that person is not around, has died or became disabled at the same time as you, or refuses to take the job? And what about the time and money it would take to get the proper authority to act on your behalf?

A durable power of attorney allows you to make the choice of who will act on your behalf in the event of incapacity, and gives that person the power immediately upon incapacity, without court action—saving time and money in the process. You can even include restrictions and directions on the exercise of the power that would not be available without this document.

What Goes into a Durable Power of Attorney?

There are three parts to a durable power of attorney: a statement of intent to create a durable power of attorney; the appointment of the attorney-in-fact/representative; and a statement of the attorney-in-fact's powers.

The good news is that all these parts can often be found in a one-page, fill-in-the-blanks form at a stationery store, or in several excellent self-help books. You can modify these forms to suit your personal needs, or use them as is.

The process is simple. Generally, all you do is sign and date the document in front of a notary public and some witnesses (a notary public and witnesses are not always required, but are recommended). There is no need to transfer title to property, as with a trust, and there are no legal reporting requirements imposed on the attorney-in-fact.

The bad news is that states can differ dramatically in their rules regarding the substance of a durable power of attorney and other requirements, like recordation. Indeed, the requirements can vary even within a state between a durable power of attorney for finance and a durable power of attorney for health care. If you're interested in pursuing this topic and cannot find a standard form sanctioned by your state, you may wish to seek the help of a local attorney experienced in such matters.

How Does a Durable Power of Attorney Interrelate with a Living Trust and a Will?

Many people with a Will and a trust don't see any reason for a durable power of attorney. What these people fail to see is that these documents provide very different functions for different times. A Will doesn't take effect until after death; a power of attorney is only good while the person is alive. You can name the same person both the executor of your Will and your attorney-in-fact, if you like, but you don't have to. In either case, the person who acts as executor will be performing different functions after your death than the attorney-in-fact will while you're alive and disabled.

A trust can and often does take effect while you're alive and provides for a change of trustees upon incapacity, but as mentioned above it only involves decision-making control over trust property, not property that may fall outside the trust, or health care decisions. Consider the following situation:

I obtained a durable power of attorney for my sister some years back before she was married. It

allows me to make financial and health care decisions on her behalf if she ever becomes disabled. After her marriage, she set up a trust and named her husband as successor trustee in the event of her death or incapacity. She never to my knowledge, however, terminated my durable power. Recently she was hit by a car and is in a coma. Under these circumstances, what say do I have?

It would appear from the facts above that this questioner has the decision-making authority for her sister's health care and for financial decisions on all assets she owns individually and outside the trust. Note that this may or may not be what her sister intended. She may have simply forgotten about the power after marriage, and wanted her new husband to have control over these decisions. Or, less likely, she may have wished her sister to make all decisions upon her incapacity, including those regarding the trust property. Whichever, this situation illustrates the need to integrate, constantly review, and update your estate plan with each change of life to make sure all the pieces continue to work well together.

How Is a Power of Attorney Terminated?

Whether a power of attorney is durable or not, it can be terminated or revoked at any time, with or without reason, by the principal—as long as the principal is competent.

What must be done to terminate a power? Simply notify the holder of the power that the power is revoked and that you no longer wish him or her to act as your attorney-in-fact. You can do this orally, but as with most things of legal significance, it's best to put it in writing. Be specific as to the power involved and send the revocation to the attorney-in-fact.

While this writing may be legally significant to terminate the power as between you and the attorney-in-fact, consider the following potential problem:

> **I gave a friend of mine a power of attorney over some property I own near where she lives so that she could sign for me during a sale. The deal, however, fell through because of some things she did, and I revoked her power. Recently, however, when I went to resell the property, I was told it was no longer in my name. Could she have sold it without my permission?**

When this questioner gave her friend the power of attorney over her real estate, it was probably recorded or in a recordable form, as is required when real estate is involved. Revoking this power may have terminated the right of the friend to transfer, but it did nothing to notify others of the change in authority. If the friend transferred the property to an innocent third party who paid valuable consideration without notice of the termination of the power (sometimes called a bona fide purchaser for value or BFP, for short), by law that person will very likely be given superior rights to the property over the original owner. Any action our caller has would then be against her friend for wrongfully taking her property.

Obviously, the moral of this story is to always revoke in writing and to notify everyone involved. In this case, the proper notification would have included a written revocation of the power recorded with the county recorders office on the property title.

Finally, it should be noted that an incompetent person cannot revoke a durable power of attorney he created, any more than he can create one. Once a person becomes incompetent, the attorney-in-fact remains in control, until recovery, death, or court order as a result of an action brought by some competent third party.

What Can Be Done to Plan for Terminal Incapacity?

With Dr. Kevorkian, sometimes referred to as Dr. Death, running around Michigan helping people with terminal illnesses die, the issue of the "right to die" has recently become a national debate. It's an issue that brings out strikingly different points of view with apparently equal fervor.

While this issue is nothing new, it has grown in importance almost certainly as a direct result of the advancements of modern medicine; advancements that can, in some cases, keep a body alive while the person is comatose without any reasonable likelihood of recovery.

To some people this is an acceptable solution, because as one friend put it: "If there is any chance that I might recover, no matter how small, put a plant on my head and keep me alive."

To others, the majority of people I've spoken with, it's quite unacceptable, because of the monetary and emotional cost to relatives and friends, or because of a belief that a life like that is no life at all.

The issue here is what you can legally do about it—especially since you'll be totally incapacitated at the time the issue arises. A couple of options are available.

First, you can give someone you trust your health care durable power of attorney with specific instructions as to what you want to happen. For example:

> **If I am ever incapacitated and kept alive on life support, I direct my attorney-in-fact to maintain life support for so long as I am alive, even if I have been diagnosed by my physician as terminally ill and unlikely to recover.**
>
> or
>
> **If I am ever diagnosed as terminally ill and kept alive on life support with no reasonable likelihood of recovery, I instruct my attorney-in-fact to order my physician to discontinue artificial life support, and to allow me to die naturally.**

Interestingly enough, while this statement may be binding on your health care attorney-in-fact, it's not binding on your doctor or the hospital that is maintaining your life. In this regard, he, she, or it may refuse to take you off life support, even when requested to do so by your attorney-in-fact. Your representative or family would then have to bring a court action to get an order terminating life support procedures in order to enforce your wishes in the matter. This is a costly, time-consuming, and emotionally draining experience at a time when family members don't need any further aggravation.

Consequently, it may be a good idea to quiz your doctor and his hospital on their views and procedures for dealing with such a situation. You might also make it known to him or her what your feelings are on the issue to help ensure cooperation when it will be most needed.

Of course, there is always the question of what is terminal, but with most doctors and hospitals erring on the side of keeping life-support going until the last possible second, there isn't much risk that it would be terminated prematurely. In any case, this is a personal decision that can only be made by you after some deep reflection.

What Is a Living Will?

Nothing is more confusing than the term *living will*. It is neither a Will nor a living trust, and really has nothing to do with either. It is actually more like a power of attorney for health care over a limited issue—terminal incapacity (the issue just discussed). A living will is simply a document that directs your doctor, attorney, and/or loved ones as to what you would like to occur if you are ever kept alive by artificial means without the reasonable possibility of recovery.

Sometimes referred to as a "directive to physician"

or a "pull-the-plug" provision, the living will is available in a majority, but not all, of the states. Consider, however, using a durable power of attorney for health care instead, if it's available where you live. The durable power of attorney allows for the appointment of a person to see that your wishes are carried out, and can be used to grant control over health decisions other than the disconnection of life support. In short, it's a much broader and more flexible instrument.

For this reason, the living will has been used less and less as the durable power of attorney becomes easier and more accepted. If you insist, you can, of course, draft both documents. Statutory forms for living wills are commonly available at stationery stores and bookstores.

What Can Be Done to Provide Income for Support During Disability?

Way back at the start of this chapter, I said you would need two things in case of disability: someone to help make your financial and health decisions, and a form of income for support. The preceding sections of the chapter discussed the first need. Now it's time to examine, briefly, the second need.

What can be done to provide income during disability? The obvious answer is insurance, specifically disability insurance. If you're ready to skip this section because you're one of the few people who still believes in the strength of the American Social Security system to take care of you in time of disability, read on. I'll spend only enough time to tell you to *think again*, unless you like living at or near the poverty level.

I report this to you only because so many of our disabled callers complain about it. The fact is that Social Security disability payments do not provide enough support to live well if you are used to living relatively well. It's a minimum payment that many people warn may not be around by the time the baby boomers reach retirement age. So if you want to have enough to live comfortably if you're ever incapacitated and cannot work, then you should check into disability coverage in addition to your Social Security benefits and regular health insurance.

CHAPTER SIX

Life Insurance

What Is Life Insurance?

In the course of a lifetime, there are few *positive* things people put off, and even avoid, more than estate planning. It has the air of death, or even disability, that makes it an unpleasant topic of consideration. Add complicated documentation that can drive even judges to their wits' end, and you have the least favorite part of this least favorite subject: life insurance.

Even people who read and write contracts for a living have trouble wading through the average insurance policy, whether life, health, or auto. It's so bad that there are laws requiring insurance companies to place a disclosure sheet on the front of many types of policies stating in short, understandable English what the policy covers. You recognize this as the only part of the policy you read (at least it's the only part of my policy I ever read).

But what is a life insurance policy, and what does it do for your estate plan?

A life insurance policy is like gambling in Vegas, except the odds are worse and winning is nowhere near as fun. You buy a policy by agreeing to pay a company (the house) money (the wager) in exchange for its agreement to pay you a sum of money if you are not alive by the end of the policy term. In short, you're betting you'll be dead before the policy period ends.

If you're right, you win, and the company pays off (not to you, of course—you're dead). If you're wrong, they rake up the money and offer you a new try.

It's no wonder that when the topic of life insurance arises people don't jump to be involved in the conversation, and no wonder that when the life insurance salesman calls, you whisper to your secretary to tell him you're out of the office until the swallows return to Capistrano. It's a boring, difficult to understand product in which you seem to lose no matter what happens.

So why do people buy life insurance? Is it those hard-selling insurance agents who never say die and take no insult personally? No, it's caution, a basic part of human nature—the part that got you reading this book about estate planning in the first place. It's the need to control or at least plan for the future and all its potential risks, even after death.

The insurance company takes some of these risks off

your back. They offer to provide cash to an estate or survivors in the event you die unexpectedly. That is not to say they take the risk of your unexpected death literally—you still die; they take the risk of loss (to a certain amount) by your unexpected death on your estate or on the people you leave behind.

This is most clearly shown in "key man" insurance situations, where an employer or a partner takes out a policy on the life of a key person on a project or job. The policy in such a situation pays the employer or partner a lump sum for losses incurred, or expected to be incurred, if that key person dies before the project is complete. If the person dies during this time, the funds can be used to cover the expenses of making the job right. The insurance company has taken a risk.

The most typical reasons to buy life insurance are to provide liquidity (cash) to pay debts, funeral expenses, taxes, or to provide support for beneficiaries. This is especially valuable if your assets are illiquid in that they cannot be turned into cash easily. Things like real estate and small self-owned businesses or partnerships are often like this. When you die, they need to be managed, paid for, or maintained in some way, and may deplete all your cash assets.

Consider the following situation:

About a year ago both of my parents died, leaving everything to my sister and myself. They had a house worth about $300,000, a building worth $1.2 million, and several partnership ventures. In all, their estate is worth almost $2 million, which my accountant estimates will cost us about

$450,000 in estate taxes. But we don't have $450,000. What can we do?

The initial answer I gave this caller was the same one she got from her accountant: sell the building. Unfortunately, she had tried this and had found the market to be so bad that she couldn't get an offer—this is the difference between an appraised property value (what it should be worth), and the real market value. The house, as it turned out, was also virtually unsalable.

So there they were, she and her sister, inheriting what most people would consider a huge estate, and yet finding themselves strapped for cash. They were, as some would say, land-poor.

At a time when these women were still dealing with the death of their parents, they shouldn't also have had to deal with the IRS and this problem. Life insurance would have been an answer, but, of course, it was too late for that. A half-million-dollar policy on one or both of the parents (not that expensive, depending on their health) would have solved this little tax issue. As it was, their only choices were to borrow against the property to pay the tax, or sell and take the loss of a forced sale.

Whether you have a $2 million or a $20,000 estate, a principal use and benefit of life insurance is to pay off your bills and give your family some needed cash after your untimely death. This benefit is that much more valuable if you're the main source of your family's income, and your death will terminate that income flow.

On the other hand, not wishing to sound like a life insurance salesman (which to me is only slightly more palatable than being a used car salesman), life insurance almost never makes mathematical sense, so don't waste your time trying to figure out if it does in coming to your decision to buy. The boys and girls of an average life insurance company, for all their Brooks Brothers and Ann Taylor suits, make the boys and girls of Las Vegas appear almost inept at the process of determining the odds (in insurance lingo: risk/reward).

This means the cost of a policy when compared to the odds of ever needing it will rarely, if ever, make sense. It will only makes sense from the standpoint of a person not wishing to take the risk of dying without funding, no matter how small that risk is, because they personally view the result as too costly if it happens.

When Should You Buy Life Insurance?

As suggested above, the time to buy life insurance is when there's a risk you don't wish to take, a risk that involves other people—usually a spouse or children. Remember, you'll be dead when the policy pays off, so if there's no one at the end of your life who needs the benefits, there's no reason to make this kind of "sucker's bet."

Thus, life insurance is not for everybody, contrary to what you might have been led to believe. It's important, generally, when two factors come together: dependents and cash needs. That is, you have dependents who will have cash needs if you die. If you have no dependents, or they will not have a need for cash when you die, you probably don't need life insurance.

Of course, you may purchase it anyway because caution is in your nature, but that is, as has been already pointed out, generally a losing bet.

What Type of Life Insurance Should You Buy?

Actually, people will rarely ask this question of the appropriate person: an independent, knowledgeable source without anything to gain by the answer. The result is usually something like the following:

> **Several months ago I bought a whole-life policy from a life insurance salesman that requires I make payments over the next five years. I really didn't understand what I was getting into when I bought the policy, but it sounded like a good idea at the time. A friend of mine pointed out that as a widow on a fixed pension this really wasn't necessary for me, and now I'm a little confused. Is a whole-life policy a good thing for me, and if not, can I get out of making these payments?**

If there is one thing for certain, in this very uncertain world, it's that if you have a mind to listen, you can have any number of life insurance salesmen you wish at your house (they will go wherever you want) explaining all the different life insurance products they sell. While such salesmen can be a wealth of information, you should constantly remind yourself that they make a commission (their living) only on what you buy, and that commission may vary greatly between different types of insurance products. This means you need to be wary of what you're told, and go into the meeting with a basic understanding of your real goals and needs before the salesman arrives.

There are basically three types of policies: term; whole life; and universal life. A term policy is what might be called *pure* insurance. It's what most people think about when they hear *life insurance*. You pay a premium (usually in one lump sum), and your estate or beneficiary gets paid a preset amount if you die within the term of the policy. It is typically cheap and simple, especially if you're young and the risk of dying within the term is low—which is why this is generally the policy of choice for young couples who want a good amount of coverage cheap.

Whole life adds to this coverage a savings feature that allows you to build up equity or what is called a "cash surrender value" in your policy. A cash surrender value is the payoff you could get if you canceled and turned in the policy. Because it's a form of cash reserve, you can also typically borrow against it—in a sense, borrow against your own money.

If you decide to borrow, however, you should be aware that the interest you pay is generally well above the interest you earn from the life insurance company. That is the business of life insurance.

The way it works is that the insurance company charges a premium well above what is needed to cover the risk of death, so they can not only cover that risk, they can put some away for you (invest it) in a type of forced savings plan—though the return or interest is generally pretty small. This excess becomes your cash reserve, which you can take or borrow against after a fixed period of time. If you cash it in, however, you're no longer insured, which is why people borrow against it.

A close look at what you buy with whole life will show the following: a recurring term policy with a savings account. However, the savings account typically pays less interest than a bank and you have no choice but to deposit and limited options on withdrawal. It's no wonder that whole life is most attractive to those who have trouble saving money on their own.

Universal life is like a whole-life policy with a more competitive return on the savings/investment portion of the policy. With universal life the company invests the surplus payment (the amount over the insurance portion) in fixed income assets such as corporate bonds, and thus pays more competitive interest rates. This also means, however, that your rate of return is not fixed as it is with whole life, and thus may drop if the market drops.

Universal life can also add an element of flexibility to your insurance coverage. It typically allows you to choose the amount of your policy payments and thus the amount of coverage from year to year. Whole life, by comparison, gives you set payments for set proceeds that cannot be varied during the policy period.

When choosing between these options, don't be surprised if you find great variation between and within individual companies as to both products. Insurance companies like to distinguish their policies for sales purposes, and the above is only a basic, bare-bones description of each type. Which one works for you will depend on your personal needs and your nature (how cautious you are).

Just remember to look carefully at what those needs are *before* buying.

Do Life Insurance Proceeds Go Through Probate?

The answer is yes and no, depending. Depending on what? Depending on who's the beneficiary of the policy.

If there is no beneficiary, or the insured decedent was the beneficiary, then the proceeds are part of the estate and must go through probate. This means the insurance company doesn't pay the proceeds to your spouse or children, they pay the probate court, which then distributes the proceeds as required by your Will.

On the other hand, if you name an individual (other than yourself) or a trust as the beneficiary of the policy, the money is transferred outside of probate directly to the beneficiary, saving time and money in the process. If your goal is to make those proceeds available to your family to cover expenses, this would be the way to go. To put it more firmly, except in rare circumstances when you may not have needed the insurance anyway, you would be stupid not to name someone other than yourself as the beneficiary of the policy.

Do Life Insurance Proceeds Get Taxed?

This question, surprisingly enough, almost never gets asked directly. Here's how it typically goes:

> *Client:* "My father died recently, and I'm trying to take care of his estate. I transferred his house into my name, collected his life insurance, took care of getting all his bank accounts closed, and handled his personal affairs. Is there anything I missed?"
>
> *Attorney:* "Have you filed the final income and estate tax returns?"
>
> *Client:* "No. Do I have to? I think he made some income before he died, but his estate is only worth about $400,000, and I was told by another attorney that this was too small of an estate to be taxed."
>
> *Attorney:* "A final income tax return should be filed if he made over the minimum amount of income during his final year of life, but you don't have to file an estate tax return if the gross estate is less than $600,000 and there are no taxes owed."
>
> [A little later in the conversation the client casually mentions that the insurance policy was for $500,000.]
>
> *Attorney:* "Did you include the policy proceeds in your calculation of the gross estate for tax purposes?"

> *Client:* "No, of course not—it came directly to me as the beneficiary. It wasn't part of his estate and didn't need to go through the probate."

As they say, herein lies the rub. What's in an estate for probate purposes is not necessarily the same as what's in an estate for estate tax purposes. In fact, it's generally far less.

The test of whether insurance proceeds are taxable as part of an estate is based on who owns the policy. If the decedent is the owner of the policy, the proceeds are part of his or her estate and thus taxable. If the decedent is not the owner of the policy, then the proceeds of the policy are not included in his or her estate for tax purposes— they're included in the estate of the actual owner. This is quite different from the probate test, where inclusion in the probate estate is based on whether the decedent's estate is the beneficiary. One asks who owns the policy, the other asks who gets the proceeds.

Some people wonder how the insured decedent, the person covered by the policy, could *not* be the owner. Again, look at the key-man type of policy, where the business or partnership buys the policy on the life of its key employee or partner. When that person dies, the proceeds go to the business. But more important, for tax purposes, is that while the person is alive the policy is paid for and controlled by the business. The insured person has no control or interest in it. Thus he or she is not the owner of the policy.

The same result can be created by an individual if that person wants to avoid having the proceeds of his life insurance policy taxed with the rest of his estate.

The test of ownership for this purpose is not a logical test, but a legal test involving several tax and legal issues concerning control over and interest in the policy. Under current tax rules these are referred to as "incidents of ownership." Incidents of ownership generally include any meaningful power over the policy, including the right to:

(1) alter, amend, or modify the policy;
(2) choose or change the beneficiary;
(3) borrow against or pledge the policy;
(4) terminate or surrender the policy; and
(5) decide which payment option will apply—lump sum or installments.

For tax purposes, the decedent is treated as owning the policy if he or she has any of these incidents of ownership.

To examine your own situation, start by asking yourself who bought the policy and/or made the payments. If you did, then you will be treated as the owner, unless you transfer the policy to someone else *without* retaining any incidents of ownership.

Thus, if you want life insurance proceeds out of your estate for probate purposes, all you have to do is name a beneficiary other than yourself. You can still own the policy, make the payments, and control its use, including reserving the right to change the beneficiary. But if you want your life insurance proceeds out of your estate for tax purposes, then you'll have to transfer all rights and ownership to someone else—meaning you lose those rights. Consider the following illustration of the potential problem here:

A couple of years back I did some estate planning and transferred my life insurance policy with a pretty good cash value to my wife. Recently we split up, and I'd like to know how I get it back.

Actually, this person's problem may not be as bad as it seems, since he may have some rights to at least part of this policy under his state divorce laws. If he had transferred the policy to his son or daughter, or brother or sister, and changed his mind, it would be too late to get it back without the other person's agreement. He would have transferred all his rights away.

I know what you're thinking. You're thinking this problem could be avoided by simply waiting until you're sick, close to death, and then making the transfer. Think again. Besides the problem of rarely knowing in advance when you are going to die and having the time to transfer an insurance policy before it happens, the Internal Revenue Code requires that the transfer, if it's a gift (someone would have to pay full value to make it not), be made more than three years before death. Any transfer of life insurance made within three years of death is disallowed for federal tax purposes. In other words, proceeds of a life insurance policy transferred within three years of death are included in the decedent's gross estate for tax purposes.

The more clever among you may be thinking like this person:

Last year I set up a living trust and transferred most of my assets into it. I intentionally left my life insurance out and named my daughter as ben-

eficiary because I wanted her to get the money directly. Only now, because of the size of my estate, I'm concerned that by doing this the life insurance will be included in my taxable estate. The problem is that my daughter is too young to get ownership of the policy right now, but what if I simply transfer ownership to my trust? Wouldn't this solve the problem?

Smart, but not smart enough. The problem is not in whose name the policy lies, but in who controls it, or more precisely, whether the decedent retains any incidents of ownership. Thus, transferring the policy to a living trust that this man controlled would not remove the policy proceeds from his gross estate for tax purposes.

There is no way around this, and people richer than us have tried. If you want your life insurance proceeds out of your estate for tax purposes, then you'll have to have someone else buy the policy with their own money, or bite the bullet and give it away more than three years before your death, keeping no strings attached.

When Should a Person Transfer a Life Insurance Policy?

There are two situations in which a person might want or need to transfer a life insurance policy: when he needs money and either sells the policy or puts it up as collateral for a loan; and when he is trying to save estate taxes. Thus, not including the former situation, the only time you'll want to transfer a policy and give up ownership and control is when you have a large enough estate, including the insurance proceeds, to be taxed.

This generally means, as we shall see in Chapter 9, an estate worth over $600,000, including the insurance proceeds, that will go to someone other than your spouse or charity. If your estate is smaller than this, or is going to your spouse, then you don't need to play the transfer game.

However, if your estate qualifies under this criterion, you still have to answer the question of whether the tax benefits are worth the loss of control and rights. This is a personal choice.

How Do You Transfer a Life Insurance Policy?

Most everyone who has a life insurance policy has the power to transfer it. The only major exception to this rule are group policies provided by employers that only allow the employer to be the owner. Otherwise the process of transferring is simple: call the insurance company and get an assignment or transfer of ownership form sent to you, then fill it out and send it back in.

Some people who don't like communicating with their insurance company for one reason or another ask if they can make this change by simply altering their Will or living trust. Unfortunately, such a change has no effect on the ownership of the policy.

You should also note that in some states designated as community property states, the rules of property ownership may make your spouse a partial owner of any life insurance policy you buy, regardless of whether he or she is registered as an owner with the company. If you live in such a state, you may be able to transfer your life insurance policy, but if you do so without your spouse's consent, then only your portion of the policy will be transferred—you can't transfer what you don't own.

If you live in a community property state, therefore, you'll need to get your spouse to sign off on any transfers or make sure the policy is a separate, noncommunity asset. (For more on this topic see in *The Five-Minute Lawyer's Guide to Divorce*.)

These laws will also affect your ability to choose a beneficiary who is not your spouse. Proceeds paid on such a policy may be claimed, partially, by your spouse even though he or she is not the named beneficiary.

Once a policy is transferred, the new owner should make all the premium payments, if any. If the original owner continues to make payments on the policy, it will appear, at least to the IRS, that he or she has retained incidents of ownership and is thus still the owner for tax purposes.

This is one reason to buy a single-premium type of policy—there are no payments after the first.

Of course, you can always give the new owner the money to make the insurance premium payments; you just can't make them directly.

Does the Gift Tax Apply to the Transfer of a Life Insurance Policy?

When someone gives someone else something of value, while they are alive, without getting something in return, there is a potential for a gift tax. While we'll be discussing this tax in more detail in Chapter 9, it's important to note here because transferring an insurance policy to another or giving someone money to pay policy premiums involves a gift that may be subject to a gift tax if it exceeds $10,000 in value.

This is not true, of course, when the transferee pays full value for the policy that is transferred. But this is the rarity, not the norm.

On the positive side, this gift tax will always be less than the tax created by the inclusion of the insurance proceeds in your estate. Why? Because the gift tax is based on the value of the policy at the time of the gift—usually the cash surrender value—while the estate tax is based on the amount of the proceeds paid out at death. And the proceeds are always going to be greater than the cash value of the policy.

Does the Recipient of Life Insurance Proceeds Have to Pay Income Taxes?

Generally no. Life insurance proceeds paid to a beneficiary after death are *not* subject to federal income taxes, either to the beneficiary who receives them or to the insured, no matter who owns the policy. Yes, I said it. Life insurance proceeds are income-tax free!

The only possible exception is interest paid on installments when the insurance proceeds are paid out over time rather than in one lump sum. In this case, the interest earned on these payments is taxable as income to the recipient (not the estate of the decedent).

What Is a Life Insurance Trust?

From time to time, you'll hear about something called a life insurance trust. Knowing from the last chapter that a trust is really just a transfer of ownership from one form to another and after reading the section above describing how transferring the ownership of a life insurance policy to a living trust will not accomplish any tax savings, you might rightly wonder what such a trust is and why someone would want to create it.

A life insurance trust is an irrevocable trust set up to own a life insurance policy. The irrevocability combined with other aspects gives it the separation from the insured it needs to avoid the incidents of ownership problem. The purpose of setting up such a trust is thus the same as transferring a life insurance policy to anyone else: to reduce estate taxes and avoid probate. And it is accomplished the same way as any other transfer, by going through the insurance company, only you must first set up the trust.

In order to make this work, however, there must be compliance with all the tax complexities discussed above. The trust must be irrevocable, established more than three years before death, and not contain any incidents of ownership. This means you, as the insured, cannot be the trustee or retain any right to alter the trust terms in any way. You must, in short, give up all control. Consider the following:

Several years back I set up a life insurance trust naming my three children as beneficiaries. Since then I have remarried and have another child on the way. How do I go about changing the trust to include this new child?

You don't. Unless all the beneficiaries (the first three children) and the trustee agree to make this change, the only thing you can do is set up a separate policy and trust for the new child.

One advantage of setting up a life insurance trust over just giving the policy to someone is that it is controlled by the trust rules, which you establish, rather than by the whims of the new owner. Thus, you could require that the policy be maintained and not cashed in during your lifetime, or that the trustee hold the proceeds until all the beneficiaries reach the age of thirty-five. Neither these nor any other restrictions could be enforced if the policy was simply transferred to someone as a gift.

CHAPTER SEVEN

Joint Tenancy with Right of Survivorship

—

What Is a Joint Tenancy with Right of Survivorship?

A joint tenancy is so deceptively simple, so apparently easy to grasp, most people feel they understand it after only a one- or two-sentence explanation. In some ways they're right, but in others they're clearly wrong.

There are two parts to a joint tenancy, the ownership part (the tenancy part) and the inheritance part (the right of survivorship part). Both are easy to explain but contain a number of far-reaching aspects that should be considered in making an estate plan. We will go over some of these aspects as we explore this ownership mechanism.

Joint tenancy is a form of ownership in which the owners hold an *undivided* interest in the entire piece of property. This means they own it together in equal shares, no owner having any right over any other owner with regard to any aspect of the property.

By far the most important distinguishing characteristic of a joint tenancy is its "right of survivorship." This is the right of a surviving owner to *automatically* inherit the interest of any co-owner who dies. For example, if there are two joint tenants and one dies, the survivor automatically owns it all. If there are three joint tenants and one dies, the remaining two each own one half, again automatically. This is the same whether there are two or twenty joint tenants; the survivors get the spoils equally.

You should already be seeing how this can affect an estate plan, but wait, it gets better; there is *no* probate process involved. *Automatically* effectively means "without probate" or any formal probate-type process. By definition, it also means without regard to what is contained in a Will or trust or any other documents. Thus, the answer to the following question is "no."

I am named as a beneficiary in my mother's Will, which gives me, among other things, her interest in a parcel of land in Las Vegas. The problem is that when I went to claim my share of the land, her brother, my uncle, said he owned it all outright since they held the property together in joint tenancy. Doesn't my right contained in the Will

take precedence over the joint tenancy, since it was made after the property was purchased?

Don't make this mistake. It's too common and unnecessary. A Will cannot dispose of joint tenancy property. *Automatically* means *automatically*, leaving nothing to be transferred by Will even when the Will specifically states otherwise. Thus, the uncle in this case got 100 percent ownership of this property upon his sister's death (regardless of her Will or her intent).

How Do You Create a Joint Tenancy?

Creating a joint tenancy in most states is largely a matter of documenting the owners' intent to create this type of ownership relationship. This is generally done in title documents, if the property is the type that requires recording of interests, like real estate, or can be done in a simple agreement between you and your co-owner if no such recording is required.

This seems simple enough, but there are a few tricks. First, the owners—all the owners—must acquire the same interest at the same time. This means that a person who owns property cannot simply transfer a portion of that property directly to another in order to create the joint tenancy. In such a case, their share of the property would have been acquired at different times.

To get around this problem, an owner of property who wishes to create a joint tenancy with another or several others simply transfers the property *to himself and the others* at the same time. Thus, if Mike Smith owned some property he wanted to share as a joint tenant with his new wife, Susan Smith, he would fill out a deed transferring the property "to Michael and Susan Smith as joint tenants with right of survivorship."

This may seem like a lot of legal mumbo jumbo, but that's only because it is. It's just another example of a legal formality created by historical accident that continues without meaning into today's world. It's not the first time we've seen such things, and it won't be the last.

You might have noticed that I not only titled this chapter Joint Tenancy with Right of Survivorship, I used this entire phrase when I described the grant in the example above. You may legitimately ask why I didn't just say *Joint Tenants* or *in Joint Tenancy:* Don't these words create a joint tenancy as well?

In some states, probably a majority, they do. But in others, historical tradition and rules of interpretation require the words *with right of survivorship* in order to create the joint tenancy relationship.

I have known several attorneys who, just to be safe, will even write *joint tenancy with right of survivorship and not as tenants in common.* This may be overly cautious, but consider the consequences if the tenancy is misinterpreted and not treated as a joint tenancy—the property does not automatically go to the joint tenant, it goes through probate. And if the Will does not contain instructions on the disposition of the property (and why should it, since the parties thought it would automatically go through the joint tenancy?), or there is no Will, the property may be passed along to someone not intended to get it. A clear case for an attorney malpractice suit, almost certainly brought by the surviving joint tenant who didn't get the property, or had to suffer through a probate process before finally getting it.

One thing, however, is for certain: simply listing the owners' names together with an *and* or an *or* is a dangerous way to try to create a joint tenancy with right of survivorship. There are a few states that allow this casual method of creating a joint tenancy, but it's not a good idea to rely on it.

In any case, remember that laws can vary from state to state, so if you intend to create a joint tenancy and want to make sure you get the benefits of the right of survivorship feature, it's a good idea to check with a title company, or an escrow or real estate lawyer in your area. For example, in some states a joint tenancy can only be created with a husband and wife. Any attempt to set up a joint tenancy outside of a legal marriage will most likely end up being treated as a tenancy in common, with all the unfortunate side effects just described.

What Kind of Property Can Be Held in Joint Tenancy?

Most people know that real estate can be held in joint tenancy but are unaware that other property, such as bank accounts and cars, can be held in this manner just as easily (if allowed by the bank and state law). Even property that is not held by another, or that does not have recording requirements for documents of title, can be held in joint tenancy, as long as the owners show an intent to do so and the law allows it.

When Should Property Be Held in Joint Tenancy?

The reason people hold property in joint tenancy is to avoid probate. And from a simplicity standpoint, it makes sense to do it in this manner. If you know who you want to give your property to when you die and that person feels the same about you, all you need to do is agree to hold as joint tenants and you've achieved your goal. The joint tenancy bypasses probate, taking no more time than buying the property in the first place. Easy.

Because of this ease of creation, joint tenancy can be particularly useful when death is imminent as a last-minute way to avoid probate. It's also a handy way to transfer property between spouses when one dies.

But even in situations such as this, there may be reasons not to hold property in joint tenancy. Here are a series of problems that consider this issue.

REASON 1:
Several years ago I transferred some property I owned into a joint tenancy with my grandson. I did it simply to avoid probate and make sure he got it when I died. Someone told me about it and it seemed simple enough. Well, now the boy has

grown up, and he says he needs the money and wants to sell his half of the property to me or someone else. I told him he doesn't own it until I die, but he insists that it's his now and he has the right. Have I made a mistake?

Maybe. This is a basic side effect of using joint tenancy for estate planning purposes—it creates co-ownership. By necessity, the person you give a joint tenancy interest to for purposes of probate avoidance gets all the rights of a co-owner *immediately*, not *after death*. If the person is not willing to go along with your wishes, he can, among other things, sell his interest, bring an action for partition to sever his interest, use the property for his own purposes, or lease it out, without your permission. He has an undivided interest in the whole and is not legally subject to your control.

But stop! The problem is even broader. Let's say the person you plan to make your joint tenant can be fully trusted to follow your wishes—can you also trust his or her creditors? Consider the following:

My sister and I own a condominium in joint tenancy we inherited from our father. We put it up for sale and in a title search I found a judgment lien had been placed on the property by one of my sister's creditors. Can they do that when it's partially my property?

Unfortunately, yes. As an owner of the property, the sister's joint tenancy interest is subject to the claims of her creditors. This doesn't mean her creditors can take both interests. They only have rights against the share owned by their debtor. They can, however, in most states take steps to obtain a court order for sale of the whole property in order to get at the debtor's interest and satisfy the debt.

But what if the joint tenant who owes the money dies before his or her creditors can come after the property?

As long as the joint tenancy wasn't set up to defraud creditors, then the death will most likely avoid their claims. Remember, the transfer is automatic at death, leaving nothing in the decedent's estate for creditors to go after. This, however, will not be the case for any creditor who has a perfected security interest, such as a recorded mortgage or judgment lien, on the property *before* the joint tenant dies.

In addition, consider that when a joint tenancy is used as a probate avoidance device, it's often expected that the transferee (the recipient of the joint interest) will live longer than the transferor (the giver of the joint interest), and it's his creditors we're concerned about. If the transferee does outlive the donor, he'll own the entire property and his creditors will be able to go after it all.

In several states, there's a form of joint tenancy called "tenancy by the entirety." A tenancy by the entirety is a marital estate, and can thus be held only by a husband and wife. Its key value, when available, is that it prohibits attachment by creditors of one of the spouses against the entire property. It doesn't stop creditors of both spouses and isn't available in all states (or even in all states that recognize the tenancy); but if you live in one of the states that recognizes and allows this sort of thing, and want to create a joint tenancy between yourself and your spouse, you may want to consider this as a form of protection against individual creditors.

Of the states that recognize a tenancy by the entirety, only the following appear to recognize this protective effect: Delaware, District of Columbia, Florida, Hawaii, Indiana, Maryland, Missouri, Pennsylvania, Rhode Island, Vermont, Virginia, and Wyoming. If you live in any of these states, check with a local attorney before attempting to set up such a tenancy to make sure this is still the law.

REASON 2:
I have a joint tenancy with two close friends, one of whom recently had a breakdown and was committed to a mental facility. The other friend and I would like to sell the property, but need the approval of our third partner to make the sale complete. How can we do this?

Once a person becomes incompetent, their signature on a contract is worthless, at least until they become competent again. They can sign, but the document is not enforceable against them. This means that the questioner will need to find a legally responsible person to agree to sign on behalf of her incompetent partner. Unless such a person has already been appointed and given authority to do so, either through a durable power of attorney or court action, the process can take a long time and possibly result in the loss of the sale.

Obviously, one way to avoid the time and cost of this process is to provide each joint owner with a durable power of attorney regarding the property. This would allow for a sale or other action by competent partners in the event one becomes disabled, yet require the signature of all if no such disability occurs.

REASON 3:
If I transfer property into a joint tenancy with a friend in order to avoid probate, will my property be reassessed for property tax purposes?

It's rare, but it can happen. In some parts of the country, a transfer of property into a joint tenancy with an independent person may cause a reassessment. Most jurisdictions, however, do not consider this a change of ownership sufficient to trigger a reassessment for property tax purposes. However, you will need to confer with local counsel or your property tax assessor to determine if this is true in your area.

In short, there are serious risks to using a joint tenancy as a probate-avoidance tool. It is one thing for people to buy property together and hold it as joint tenants because they want the other to get their interest if they die. It is a whole other thing to take property that is solely owned and transfer it into joint tenancy with another simply to avoid the probate process. By doing so, you effectively give away an interest in the property that may be sold, attached by creditors, tied up if the person becomes incapacitated, or even reassessed for property tax purposes. For a co-owner who puts in only a portion of the cost of the property, this is all part of the normal risk of sharing ownership. For a sole owner of property wishing only to create a device to transfer the property after death, this may add significant risks that do not make sense under the circumstances.

Can You Get Property Back Once You've Transferred It into Joint Tenancy as a Gift?

Not without the agreement of the recipient. As they say, a gift given is gone. For this reason in particular, many people prefer a revocable living trust to a joint tenancy as a probate-avoidance device.

How Do You Sever or Break a Joint Tenancy?

What happens when a joint tenant no longer wants his co-owner to inherit his portion of the property? Can he, as we say in legal circles, sever the joint tenancy?

The answer is yes, easily, without even consulting the other co-owner.

How is this done?

In every state a joint tenancy can be broken simply by transferring the property to any other person.

What if you can't find a buyer or don't want to sell?

Selling the joint tenancy interest is only one way to sever. You can, in many states—but not all—simply transfer it to a person known as a straw man, who immediately transfers the property back to you. If you're concerned that the straw man won't transfer the property back, you can have the process handled through an escrow or attorney's office. Lawyers commonly do this for their clients, having themselves or their secretary play straw man. In some states, California, for example, you can even quit-claim the property to yourself with a statement of your intent to sever the joint tenancy—but don't try this without legal help. The key is to transfer the property and record the transaction before death.

Once severed, the one-time joint tenancy interest is held as a tenancy in common. If there is more than one other tenant, the other tenants will continue to hold as joint tenants between themselves, but not as to the tenant who severed. This means that when the tenant who severed dies, his interest will *not* automatically go to the other tenants, and conversely, when they die, their interest will *not* automatically go to the severed joint tenant.

If joint tenancy can be terminated so easily by either tenant without the consent of the other, what do you do if one joint tenant terminates a joint tenancy and you don't want it terminated?

Too bad; it's terminated. If a joint tenant no longer wants to hold with a right of survivorship, there's no way to stop the severance. Of course, the parties are still co-owners of the property—as tenants in common—just without survivorship benefits. You may also wish to note that even this co-ownership relationship can be terminated by either party through a "partition action." A partition action is a lawsuit requesting the court to divide the property between the owners (so they become individual owners of separate pieces, rather than undivided owners of the whole), or to sell the property in a forced sale and divide the proceeds.

Is a Transfer of a Joint Tenancy Interest Subject to Gift Taxes?

A transfer of a joint tenancy interest *without* adequate consideration (exchange of value) is a gift. If the value of the interest is over $10,000 (the federal gift tax annual exclusion), the gift is subject to gift taxes.

Thus, no gift tax would apply between joint purchasers if each were to put up their fair share of the purchase price, or the value of the interest given was less than $10,000. However, if a sole owner gives, without any return value, a joint tenancy interest worth more than $10,000 in order to avoid probate, the transfer is a gift subject to federal gift and estate taxes.

In addition, you should note that the $10,000 annual gift tax exclusion is cumulative in the sense that it can be exceeded by making a number of gifts to a single person that total more than $10,000. The key words are *to a single person*. Multiple gifts *to* different persons, or *from* different people, do not get added together.

Consequently, a husband and wife can each make $10,000 gifts to each of their three children for a total value of up to $60,000 ($20,000 each child) without gift tax consequences. However, if they were to give all $60,000 to only one child, they would have made a taxable gift and be required to file a gift tax return.

If this limit on tax-free gifts has you concerned, don't panic yet. As will be more fully explained in Chapter 9, the fact that a gift tax return must be filed, or even that a taxable gift has been made, doesn't mean a tax must be paid. Accessed taxes are deducted against a uniform gift and estate tax credit of $600,000 in a lifetime, meaning that gift taxes are not owed until you've made more than $600,000 in total noncharitable gifts—over and above the $10,000 annual exclusion—in a lifetime.

There is an exception for gifts between husbands and wives, who currently can make unlimited gifts between themselves without gift or estate tax consequences.

Another exception occurs when a person sets up a bank account or buys a savings bond and adds another person's name to the account. This is treated by the IRS as an *incomplete* gift that only becomes a complete and therefore taxable gift when the donee takes possession of the money—for example, by withdrawal.

Note that, for tax purposes, a gift is made whether the property is *transferred* from a sole owner into joint tenancy at no cost, or *purchased* using the money of one person but put in the name of another jointly.

What Are the Federal Estate Tax Effects of Setting Up a Joint Tenancy?

Unlike the advantages of avoiding probate, there are no federal estate tax savings generated by setting up a joint tenancy, and in fact there may be some dangers.

As we saw in the chapter on life insurance, there are really two different estates: a probate estate and a taxable estate; and the rules for determining the taxable estate clearly cover a broader range of the decedent's property. Thus, when a joint tenant dies, his or her share of the property may avoid probate and automatically go to the surviving joint tenants, but that share is still part of his or her taxable estate.

All right, you say, I can live with that—if I'm a joint tenant and die first, the value of my interest in the property is included in my estate for tax purposes. But stop! It may not be just your interest in the property that's included. A joint tenant's interest for tax purposes may or may not be equal to the interest actually owned by that joint tenant (whether one half, one third, or one quarter).

Getting confused and a little concerned? You are dealing with the IRS now, not the probate court.

A decedent's taxable interest in joint tenancy property is not based on ownership in the traditional sense, it's based on how much of the purchase price—plus cost of improvements—the decedent put into the property. Thus, if the decedent put up the entire purchase price for a piece of property, the full value of the property is included in his gross estate for tax purposes.

But wait, there's more good news from our taxing authorities.

In determining what interest should be included in a decedent's gross estate for tax purposes, the IRS does an interesting thing, not surprising for the IRS: it *presumes* the first joint tenant to die paid the entire cost of purchase and improvements.

Do you see the hidden danger here? If the presumption holds, the entire value of the asset is included in the decedent's gross estate and then again in the surviving joint tenant's gross estate when he dies.

Before I scare you too much, I should let you know this is a rebuttable presumption—a presumption that can be proved false by producing evidence that the surviving joint tenant provided his share, or all, of the costs and expenses of obtaining or improving the property. If the surviving joint tenant paid the entire purchase price of the property, none of its value will be included in the decedent's estate.

The moral: Keep complete records on property purchases, especially when holding them in joint tenancy.

As far as married couples are concerned, the rule is that one half of the value of joint tenancy property is included in the estate of the first spouse to die, no matter who paid for the property. In such a case, there is little if any tax effect from including the one-half interest in the estate, since there is an unlimited marital deduction for estate transfers going to one's spouse (see discussion in Chapter 9).

What Are the Federal Income Tax Effects of a Joint Tenancy?

You would think none, other than the joint tenant's share of profits and losses proportionate to ownership (as more traditionally defined). But this isn't strictly true. There's a hidden potentially negative income tax effect on the survivor because of something called the "stepped-up basis rule."

Under federal income tax laws, taxable gain on the sale of property is determined by subtracting the property's "basis" (cost for tax purposes) from its sale price.

Thus, the more the basis, the less the gain (and so the tax) on sale. Normally, basis is determined by adding the cost of purchasing the property to any improvements made, and then subtracting depreciation (if any). When a person inherits property, however, the basis is said to get a "step-up" (increase) equal to the fair market value of the property at the date of the decedent's death. This can create wonderful tax benefits for the survivor, as the following example shows:

Let's say you purchased your house, back when houses were affordable, for $50,000. (Yes, for those readers who are under forty, there was a time when this was possible.) You held it. You lived in it. Your kids grew up in it, and you put another $40,000 into it in improvements: a pool, a new roof, an add-on rumpus room, and the like. Because it's your personal home, you took no depreciation on it. What is your basis? It's $50,000 + $40,000 = $90,000. (Keep good records!)

Now, let's further assume that if you wanted to sell this home today you could get $240,000, net costs of sale. If you actually did sell it, you would determine your gain by taking the sale price (less costs of sale), which is $240,000 in this example, and simply subtracting the basis, $90,000. This gain, $150,000 ($240,000 − $90,000), would be taxable income to you in the year of sale (assuming you don't have a way to defer or avoid this tax).

If, however, instead of selling the house, you died owning it and transferred it through your Will or a trust to your son and daughter, the basis of the property to your children (because of the step-up) would be its fair market value at the date of your death, or $240,000. Thus, if the children decided to sell right after your death, they would have no gain because the basis would equal the sale price—assuming they can get the fair market value. A much nicer result.

The logic behind this step-up rule is that when an asset passes from a decedent it gets included, and thus taxed, at its fair market value. Consequently, it should be treated as having passed to the beneficiaries at that amount. But the property may not have actually been taxed at all, if, for example, the estate was less than $600,000.

The problem with regard to a joint tenancy (as shown in the last section) is that not all of the property is always included in the decedent's gross estate, and only the part that is gets a step-up in basis. Thus, if the entire value of the property was included in the decedent's estate, then the property would have a step-up in basis to the current fair market value. But if only half of the value of the property is included in the decedent's estate, only one half of the property's basis will be increased to its current value.

Using the example above, let's say you die and your spouse (rather than your children) receives your share of the property as a joint tenant through a right of survivorship, instead of by Will. As a result, she would get a step-up in basis on your half of the property only. The basis of her half, since she didn't inherit it, would remain as before. If she then sold the property shortly after you died, her taxable gain would be determined as follows:

$240,000	sale price
−45,000	regular basis of ½ the property
−120,000	stepped-up basis for ½ the property
$75,000	gain for tax purposes

Better than if you had sold together before death, but not as good as if she had gotten a step-up in basis on the full value of the property.

Note that this result may change in community property states—states that maintain community property rules for married couples. Community property states include: Arizona, California, Idaho, Nevada, New Mexico, Texas, Washington, and Wisconsin. According to the Internal Revenue Code, when one spouse dies and the other gets community property, the surviving spouse gets a step-up in basis on the *entire* value of the property. This is an added bonus for those of you in community property states, so don't forget to maintain records that show the property was community owned. You can do this either by signing an agreement between you and your spouse that the property is community, or by recording the title as: "John and Mary Smith, community property held in joint tenancy with right of survivorship." Note, however, title companies will sometimes refuse to insure this form of title, for reasons that are not often made clear.

You might also want to consider that the step-up in basis rule is in direct conflict with the goal of reducing the size of an estate for estate tax purposes. For purposes of the rule, you want property included in your estate so as to get the step-up in basis, but by doing so the value of the property becomes taxable as part of the estate, if the estate exceeds $600,000. Consequently, taking advantage of the step-up in basis rule works best for highly appreciated property that is part of a relatively small estate (under $600,000, including the property), or is going to a spouse so that the unlimited marital deduction can be used to reduce any estate tax impact caused by the inclusion of the property in the estate. We will discuss this conclusion in more detail in Chapter 9.

How Do You Obtain Full Title to Joint Tenancy Property After Your Joint Tenant Dies?

While title automatically vests in the surviving joint tenants, the survivors still need to perform a few cleanup procedures to clear the decedent's name off the official records (wherever they are). This doesn't mean a probate procedure, but it does generally require the filing of a death certificate and other documents, such as an affidavit, to establish the survivor as the sole owner. Documents needed for this purpose can be obtained from the attending physician or hospital that recorded the death, and from the recorder of documents or even certain self-help books.

CHAPTER EIGHT

Gifts to and Care of Minor Children

All questions we receive at Tele-Lawyer sound important, but few seem to have the significance of the one question every parent wants answered: If I die, what will happen to my children?

In the estate planning arena, there are two things that should be done with regard to minor children in the event something happens to both parents: a plan for the children's care, and a plan for the management of their property or finances. A precondition is that both parents are dead or incapacitated before these plans are put into effect. The assumption is that if one parent is alive, the kids will be cared for under that parent's direction. Another assumption in this chapter is that the children we're discussing are underage minors (generally under eighteen years of age), and thus not competent to care for themselves.

What Can Be Done to Provide for the Care of Your Minor Children in the Event You Die or Become Incompetent?

For obvious reasons, single parents seem to have this concern even more than married ones. They want to know who will take care of their minor child if something happens to them. *Something* may mean being hit by a bus, or having a stroke or heart attack that disables the parent. Consider this situation:

> **My sister was recently killed in a car accident. She had no Will or anything like that, but a few years ago she wrote me a letter asking if I would take care of her two children if something ever happened to her. Her husband is not alive either, and other than my mother, I am her closest living family. Will I get custody of the children if my mother fights me?**

The question here is, between two close relatives, who will get custody of the kids when both parents are dead? The answer is whoever can provide, in the court's judgment, the best environment for raising the children. If you know anything about divorce, this may sound ominously familiar. In fact, it's the same test used by courts for the determination of custody in a custody battle, also known as the "best interests of the children test."

Understandably, parents have a right to be concerned about such a decision. One of the last things a child needs after losing both parents, whether through death or disability, is to have relatives fighting over custody. In the situation posed above, the mother sent a letter to her brother (the caller) to voice her choice of custody. This letter is nice as an indication of the mother's preference at the time she wrote it, but it is not a legal document. A custody decision is made based on all the facts and circumstances concerning the best interests of the children at the time of the court hearing on the matter. Things like where the children will live; in what kind of community; what is the person's history with raising children, stability at the job, financial ability to provide support, temperament, personal habits, and the like are all examined in light of the needs of the children before a final decision can be made.

One way to avoid a dispute in this area is to make the choice yourself, before you die, in your Will. While not always binding on a court, such a declaration has a much greater effect on a court's decision than a mere letter or other informal instrument. It's also an excellent idea to have a talk with your close relatives, telling them what you would like to happen and the reasons why. At such a time, it's wise to get everyone's agreement, especially the person you intend to choose.

Choosing an alternate guardian for the children, by the way, isn't a bad idea either. It covers your child's care if the first person is unable or unwilling to serve, and allows the court a second choice, if there's a dispute.

There are two things to remember when appointing a personal guardian for minor children:

(1) *You can only name your choice for personal guardian of your minor child in a Will.* This means that a trust or a letter is not the appropriate place to attempt to name a guardian, and certainly the executor or trustee are not automatic choices for the job. You should name the guardian in a specific statement in the Will, declaring your reasons for making the choice, if any. If nothing else, this gives you at least one good reason to have a Will, even if you have a trust.

(2) *Your choice is not automatic.* This is a crucial point. You can name a choice for guardian in your Will, but a court doesn't have to agree and the person named doesn't have to accept. This is one of those subtle problems that requires flexibility. You may name the person you want to be guardian, but then that person dies, becomes an alcoholic, or leaves and cannot be found. All sorts of reasons exist why, when the need arises, the person you named may not be right or best for the children. A court, therefore, retains the power to make a decision different from the one you have made, and, of course, the person named retains the right to refuse the responsibility.

However, just because a court doesn't have to choose the person you name as guardian doesn't mean you shouldn't bother to include such a declaration in your Will. You most definitely should. As a practical matter, the judge will almost always appoint the person you choose, unless there is a challenge and the challenge is strongly based on the competence of the person named.

This brings us to an important point. I said a few paragraphs back that one of the last things the kids need is to have adults fighting over their custody after losing their parents. Actually, this is the second to last thing. The last thing is to not have anywhere to go. Consider this:

> **I am a thirty-year-old single parent of three children, and I have been trying to prepare a Will for the benefit of my children. My problem is that my only living relative, my father, is an alcoholic who abused me as a child and is too old, in any case, to handle my children. I don't want them to go through what I went through. I want to make sure if anything happens to me they are taken care of by someone other than him. What can I do?**

Here it is, the situation every parent dreads: no responsible adult to take care of the kids. If something were to happen to this woman (and her father was truly incompetent), what would become of the children? The answer: The state would assume responsibility and they'd be raised in a foster home or orphanage and put up for adoption. Moreover, while most state authorities try to keep brothers and sisters together, this is not always possible, and the kids could be split up.

No loving parent wants any of this for their children.

So what can you do? Make friends, good friends, if you have no family. People you can trust who care about your kids. This can be as much a part of an estate plan as drafting a Will or making a trust. Don't get me wrong, I'm not saying you should make friends just to have someone to foist your children on if something happened to you. The idea is to make friends for your life, and if this means that you have, at the same time, formed a relationship with an adult who would be ready, willing, and able to take on the care of your children if something happened to you, so much the better. If you have such a friend, ask him or her if it's okay to name them in your Will. Get their consent and involvement so you can be more assured they will serve if the time ever comes.

Can Two People Be Appointed as Joint Guardians?

It's surprising how many people feel they must name a couple, and not just one person, as joint guardians of their minor children. Actually, my advice is to always name an individual as guardian, rather than a couple, even if that individual has a spouse. Why? Because couples get divorced, or they can't agree on how to raise the kids. Name the person you want, the one you most trust to make the right decisions, and then the couple can work out their respective roles between them.

Can a Parent Name Someone Other Than the Other Parent as Guardian of Their Minor Child?

This is a complex question that is so commonly asked it's scary. The situation is as follows:

> I am divorced with custody of my two children. Recently I decided to draft a Will and noticed there was a provision in the form for appointment of a guardian. What I want to know is, can I name someone other than my ex-husband? He's a complete idiot who can't keep a job, let alone take care of the kids. I would like to name my brother, who has a nice, stable family with two kids and a good job. Since I was given sole custody in the divorce, would there be any problem with doing this?

You can name whoever you want in your Will, but once again, there's no guarantee your choice will be followed if challenged. In fact, the general rule is that a court will give custody to a parent before anyone else, unless the parent has abandoned the children, or is found to be unfit.

Getting sole custody does not give a parent the right to will children away from their other parent. Thus, the fact that the mother in this question got custody as a result of the divorce is largely irrelevant, except as to any underlying evidence that shows the father is unfit. This was simply a choice between two parents. If the custodial parent dies or becomes disabled, the strong preference of a court will be to place the children with the remaining parent.

Consider also that it's very difficult to prove a parent is unfit or has abandoned the children. Most people who ask this type of question detest their ex-spouse, find them irresponsible or untrustworthy, but this doesn't make them unfit. Similarly, the fact that they show up late for visitations or have visited only infrequently does not generally amount to abandonment.

Before you decide to embark on creating a situation like this, which may very well lead to a custody battle following your death, you may want to talk the situation over with the person you plan to appoint. Give him or her your reasoning and make sure he or she is willing to walk into the legal dispute and hassle. More importantly, look at the reality of the situation and make sure it's not just your prejudice and anger motivating this decision.

Situations when it makes sense to name someone other than the children's natural parent as guardian, even though that parent is alive, include:

(1) The parent is nowhere to be found, or hasn't been heard from in over a year (although you and the kids have been in a place where the other parent could find you).
(2) The parent is incarcerated.
(3) The parent has been charged with and/or has a tendency toward child abuse—physical, sexual, or mental.
(4) The parent is an alcoholic or drug abuser who has not worked out his or her problems.

(5) The parent is mentally incompetent, subject to seizures, or unable to function because of mental illness.

There are, no doubt, other situations, but these are the most pressing. The important thing is to make sure the reason is real as well as significant, and then, as with any case of naming a guardian who may later be challenged, you:

(1) prepare a Will with the person you want named as the guardian; and
(2) provide a detailed explanation of your reasoning either in the Will or in a separate letter attached to the Will.

Does the Same Person Have to Be the Guardian for All the Children?

No. But, then again, do you want your children split up? Siblings generally need each other more than ever when a parent has died, making different guardians a bad idea. Sometimes, however, this can't be helped, as in the case where there are too many children for one guardian to easily handle, or when the children have different fathers and the fathers are still alive.

What Should Be Done to Provide for the Financial Future of Your Children in the Event You Die?

The other half of "what will become of the children?" is what can be done about their financial situation after your death.

> **"How can I make sure my children can afford to live comfortably, if I die tomorrow?"**

> **"How can I provide for my child's future college education, if I'm not around?"**

The answer starts with choosing a person to manage your children's inheritance while they're still legally children. This person is often the same person you've chosen to be the kids' personal guardian, but need not be. There may be one person you think will be better able to raise the kids, make the right decisions for their education and health, provide a good home, and furnish the moral guidance you would have provided, and a different person you think is better able to understand and take care of the legacy you leave your children.

Either way, because children cannot generally manage and control property (most states allow children to own property only up to a certain dollar amount or value, usually under $5,000), there needs to be a competent adult assigned to handle the task. Choose this person with the same care as you would a trustee of a trust (as discussed in Chapter 4). He or she will be fulfilling the same sort of functions.

The second half of providing for the financial future of your children is to make sure there's enough money for them to live comfortably when you're not around. Of course, you could rely on the personal guardian to provide this support, and in many cases the person you choose will be willing to do so. However, this may just as easily not be true, and certainly might be considered unfair in the larger scheme of things.

There are two solid methods of creating a pool of cash to cover the cost of raising your kids if you cannot do so: savings, and life insurance. Saving is a matter of income and lifestyle, and if you can do it, the money can obviously be used for other things if nothing happens to you before your children can care for themselves.

Life insurance, at least pure life insurance, as discussed in Chapter 6, is faster and created exactly for this purpose. It is often a young couple's best method of ensuring funds for their child's care and education in the case of their untimely death.

One thing to consider when buying life insurance for this purpose is how to get the proceeds to your children. This may seem easy at first, by simply naming them beneficiaries of the policy or transferring the policy to them outright. These solutions not only achieve the goal of getting insurance proceeds to the children, they avoid probate and possibly estate taxes.

You should note, however, that there's a hidden danger in doing these things. An insurance company often cannot or will not give the proceeds to the children outright, because of the laws on minors owning property. It will therefore insist on distributing the money to the children's legal guardian as appointed by a court of law following a court proceeding.

After all we've discussed in this book and what you know innately, you should sense the difficulties this can create. First there will need to be a court proceeding, with all its associated costs and fees. Then there will be the need for continued court supervision over the person named as guardian, which will mean restrictions on how the guardian can act as well as an additional expense of court supervision and reporting.

Such court supervision can be beneficial in the event you don't fully trust the person handling the children's estate, but if this is the case, you may want to avoid the negative consequences of court supervision by choosing another method of leaving insurance proceeds, as well as other property, to your children, such as a trust (discussed below).

Can a Trust Be Used to Manage My Child's Inheritance?

Yes. In many cases a trust will provide the most secure and flexible method for obtaining ongoing supervision of your child's money.

Sometimes called a "children's trust," or a "trust for minors," this instrument is nothing more than a trust set up for the settlor's minor children. Consequently, the same rules and caveats apply to this trust as for any trust, with the minor (excuse the pun) distinction that the beneficiaries in such an instrument are under age.

In fact, if you've already established a living trust as part of your estate plan, you need not create a separate trust for this purpose. All that needs to be done is to provide for the appointment and duties of a successor trustee with regard to the portion of trust properties held for the minor children.

This usually means the creation of restrictions on how the trustee can invest trust property and when he can distribute money. Typically, the trustee, for example, can only invest in "conservative" investments as part of his or her trust duties: things like bonds and bank CD's, rather than wildcat oil- and gas-drilling limited partnerships. In addition, the trustee is often limited to disbursing trust income or property only for the child's health, education, general welfare, or living accommodations, and prohibited from making a final distribution of trust property until the child reaches an age specified by the settlor. The trustee, depending on how much you trust him or her, can be given broad discretion to determine what is in the child's best interest in distribution decisions.

The following are several basic questions that commonly arise in this subject area:

Is It a Good Idea to Set Up Separate Trusts for Each Child? Can Each Trust Be Managed by Different Trustees?

You can do this, but it does add some costs and complications to the process. The more trustees and separate trusts there are, the more duplication of paperwork and fees.

Should I Establish My Children's Trust in My Will?

You can do this, but the property will then have to go through probate with all its accompanying delays and costs. Therefore, setting up a living trust with provisions for the children in the event you die (a form of subtrust) is often the better solution.

If a Trust Distributes Property to Children When They Turn a Certain Age, What Happens When There Are Several Children of Different Ages?

You have two choices: each child can get his or her pro rata share as they reach the chosen age of eighteen or above; or all children can receive the proceeds at the same time when the youngest reaches the age of choice. This latter choice works best when you don't wish to divide the trust into separate distributions.

What Are the Disadvantages and Limitations of Using a Trust to Manage Children's Property?

The disadvantages and limitations of a minor's trust are the same as for trusts generally. If the property is not in the trust, actually owned by the trust, it cannot be managed by the trustee. This means things that are not transferred into the trust, because they're forgotten or cannot be transferred because they're not owned by the settlor yet, must be transferred in or handled by the Will.

A more particular problem is cost. It costs to manage trust property; not as much as having court supervision over a guardian, but it does cost. In addition, there is the paperwork, including record keeping and tax return filings, making a trust a somewhat expensive way to go. Consequently, before deciding to create a minor's trust, make sure the property being put in it justifies the time and money necessary to maintain it. Generally, you may want to consider other methods of handling this situation if the total value of trust property is less than $100,000.

What Methods, Other Than a Trust, Can Be Used to Leave Property to Children?

The simplest method is to just leave the property to your children under the supervision of a chosen guardian in your Will. This is simplest in the sense that it's the easiest to set up. You just name the guardian in the Will, providing what restrictions you want in that document. This allows you to make a choice of guardian and lay out some rules about raising the children and spending their (your) money, without having to go through any more of a formality than drafting a Will.

On the other hand, this simple method of setup doesn't typically end in the simplest, cheapest, or easiest method of implementing the estate plan. As mentioned above, when using this method, the property goes through probate and the guardian is subject to court rules and restrictions. This may mean a requirement of court approval before making expenditures of funds, and/or an obligation to provide the court with regular reports, all with the accompanying time delays and costs.

Another alternative is to leave property to your children under the Uniform Transfers to Minors Act (UTMA). The UTMA is a proposed set of laws developed by a group of legal scholars and designed to lay out how the law "should" be regarding transfers to minors. Thus, the term *uniform* does not indicate that the law is actually uniform, but how the law should be made uniform.

The fact is, a majority of but not all states have passed the basic provisions of the UTMA. (For a listing, see the chart on page 175). In addition, many states that have adopted the Act have made substantial changes to the "uniform" provisions, in effect putting their individual stamp on the statute.

What does the UTMA do? The Act allows you to leave property to a minor either by Will or through a trust by specifying a custodian who is responsible for supervising the property. This is done simply by naming the property, minor, and custodian in the Will or trust, and stating that the custodian is to act under the Uniform Transfers

**States That Have Passed
the Uniform Transfers to Minors Act**

Alabama	Illinois	New Hampshire	Oregon
Arizona	Iowa	New Jersey	Rhode Island
Arkansas	Kansas	New Mexico	South Dakota
California	Kentucky	North Carolina	Virginia
Colorado	Maine	North Dakota	West Virginia
District of Columbia	Massachusetts	Ohio	Wisconsin
Florida	Minnesota	Oklahoma	Wyoming
Hawaii	Missouri		
Idaho	Montana		
	Nevada		

to Minors Act of your state. If your state doesn't have such an Act, then you generally cannot make a gift to your minor in this manner.

The UTMA sets forth rules regarding the custodian's duties and powers that in many ways make the custodian like a trustee of a trust. The major difference is that a custodian under the UTMA is not required to file a separate tax return—everything goes on the minor's tax return, unlike a minor's trust. There is no separate legal entity.

On the other side, a transfer under the UTMA is less flexible than a trust. The reason is that several things you can decide when creating a trust are decided for you under the UTMA. For example, under the UTMA a child must usually receive the property by either the age of eighteen or twenty-one—in one case twenty-five—depending on the state. Also, unlike a trust, there can only be one custodian and one donee, and specific restrictions on the custodian's powers cannot be created; the UTMA provides for broad discretion of the custodian.

A gift under the UTMA is therefore most advantageous when the inheritance is relatively small (generally under $100,000), and thus does not justify the use and control of an ongoing trust. It provides the benefit of broad control without the difficulty and cost of creating a separate entity.

Moreover, a gift under the UTMA can be used to avoid the court supervision, bond, and resulting paperwork of a direct gift to a minor child through a guardian named in a Will.

CHAPTER NINE

Gift, Estate, and Inheritance Taxes

Typically, a chapter about taxes in an estate planning book would simply be entitled "Taxes." I titled this chapter differently to emphasize a point—there are several different kinds of taxes to be concerned about when creating an estate plan, the least of which is the one almost everyone thinks about first when they hear the word *taxes:* income tax.

Of course, income taxes do play a part in the estate *handling* process. For example, a decedent is taxed on the income he earned up till his death. Then, after death, there may be income earned, and thus income taxes owed, by the decedent's estate—dead persons do not earn income.

Still, while these taxes must be accounted for and paid, they are not really part of an estate *plan*. They're just part of the cleanup process that occurs after someone dies.

The taxes we're most concerned with for estate planning purposes are federal and state gift and estate taxes, and state inheritance taxes. We will generally concentrate here on federal law, as only seven states—Delaware, Louisiana, New York, North Carolina, South Carolina, Tennessee, and Wisconsin—have a gift tax, and in the seventeen states that have state inheritance or estate-type taxes the tax is generally of limited effect (see page 206). If you live in one of these states and are planning on making a large gift, you may want to look into your potential state gift or inheritance tax liability by contacting local counsel.

Here are the premier questions people want answered regarding these types of taxes.

What Is a Gift Tax?

Here's a typical question regarding the gift tax:

> **My father wants to give me $5,000, but both he and I are concerned that this will be subject to a gift tax. Is it, and if so, how is it paid?**

It's not, at least for this amount.

A gift tax is simply a tax that applies, under certain circumstances, when you give anything worth value to another. To give in this context means to transfer property for a noncommercial purpose for less than its full value. One question here is your intent: did you intend to make a gift of all or part of the property transferred, or did you just make a bad bargain and get less than the fair market value for the property?

While this is easy to say, it's not always easy to discern from a set of facts. For example, let's say you just transferred your business to your son for $48,000, payments to be made at a rate of $1,000 per month for the next 48 months. Have you made a gift? Maybe, if the business was worth $148,000.

The determination is made by looking at the *objective* evidence created by all the facts and circumstances surrounding the transfer. Was it made to a relative? Close friend? What was received in exchange for the property? How was the value determined?

All kinds of transfers that you may not think of as a gift may be considered to be so for gift tax purposes: making an interest-free or low-interest loan; creating an irrevocable trust for another; forgiving someone's debt; or transferring a home into joint tenancy with another. Any time you transfer anything (while you're still alive) to another and receive less than full value for the property, there is a reasonable likelihood that the transaction will be considered a gift or partial gift.

What Are the Exclusions and Deductions from the Gift Tax?

In the question stated above, the proposed transfer is clearly a gift from the father to the son of $5,000. Even so, this is not subject to gift taxes because there is a $10,000 annual exclusion.

On its face this exclusion appears simple enough: everyone gets to give away up to $10,000 to any person they want, each year, gift tax free. Still, there are several questions that often get raised.

I have two children. Can I give $10,000 to each child each year, or do I have to divide the $10,000 between them?

The rule is $10,000 per year, per person, and there is no limit on the total amount that can be given away (except your assets). Thus, if this person had five children, he could give $10,000 each for a total of $50,000. Moreover, if he had three friends he wanted to give $10,000 each (and who wouldn't want a friend like this?), he could do that as well, all gift tax free.

In addition, if he was married and his wife wanted to join in on the giving, they could jointly give up to $20,000 to each child and friend annually.

What is the benefit of all this generosity in estate planning terms? Very simply, it gets assets out of your estate, avoiding estate taxes when you die.

Of course, making gifts like this for estate planning purposes is silly unless you really want the person on the other end to get the money or the property. Remember, even taxed at the top rates, the $10,000 will only cost the estate $5,500, leaving a net positive to be transferred after death of $4,500. If you transfer this money while you're alive, you lose the use of the *entire* amount immediately, all to protect against some future estate tax that may never be owed. The point is not to avoid making gifts, but to have a reason for it beyond taxes.

I know what you're thinking. You're thinking: "Hey, I can reduce my estate taxes just before death, not to mention get money out of probate, by making a series of $10,000 gifts before I die." Unfortunately, even if you were lucky—or unlucky—enough to know when you were going to die so you could execute this plan, the IRS has got you covered with the "transfers within three years of death" rule. Under this rule, any gifts made within three years of a person's death are added back into his estate for estate tax purposes. This includes gifts under $10,000.

The effect of this rule can be quite substantial. For example, you might remember the earlier suggestion about making a gift of a life insurance policy to reduce estate taxes. The concept was to transfer the policy to the beneficiary so it was outside the insured's estate and not owned by him for tax purposes. There is a gift, no question, unless the beneficiary or recipient pays full value for the policy, but the value of the gift is almost always going to be substantially less than the value of the policy if it pays out. Why? Because a policy is generally worth far less when there is only a likelihood of having to pay out, than when the money is actually issued at full coverage.

This plan goes out the door for tax purposes (you still avoid probate) if the gift is made within three years of death, because the IRS considers the policy part of the estate.

On occasion, we'll get a concerned call from a parent like the following:

> **For the past few years I've been paying my daughter's college education and never thought a moment about it. Recently, however, a friend informed me that since she's an adult and the cost is over $10,000, this may be considered a gift subject to federal gift taxes. How can this be?**

It can't, and it isn't. In addition to the $10,000 annual exclusion, there is also an exemption for gifts made for school tuition. Thus, a parent who wants to cover the cost of his child's college education can do so without fear of tax implications. Note also that a similar exemption exists for medical expenses.

In addition to the above exclusions and exemptions, there is an unlimited *deduction* for any gifts made to a spouse or bona fide tax-exempt charitable organization. This means you can give as much as you like to your spouse or a tax-exempt charity, without gift tax liability, as long as you are legally married or the charity has tax-exempt status.

In this regard, it's worth your time to confirm the tax-exempt status of any organization you plan to make a gift to, and it might not be a bad idea even to confirm whether you're legally married. In most situations, this will be simple, but in others it may not. Consider the following:

I have been living with someone for the past seven years. We have never gone through a legal ceremony or gotten a license, but we consider ourselves married. If he makes a gift to me of a car, will there be a gift tax?

The answer to this depends on the laws of the state where the couple resides. There are several states that recognize common-law marriage, which is a marriage created by living together and holding yourself out as husband and wife without an official state license. These states include Alabama, Colorado, District of Columbia, Georgia, Idaho, Iowa, Kansas, Montana, Ohio, Oklahoma, Pennsylvania, Rhode Island, South Carolina, and Texas. If you live in one of these states, or even did live in one long enough to meet the criteria for a common-law marriage, then you may be treated as married for gift *and* estate tax purposes, and can use the unlimited marital deduction. If not, you're probably not married—at least for tax purposes—no matter how you feel about each other, and this deduction will be denied.

It should also be noted that this unlimited marital deduction does not apply to gifts to a spouse who is not a U.S. citizen, and it doesn't matter that he or she may be living in this country as a legal resident. For non-U.S.-citizen spouses there is a $100,000 annual exclusion for gift tax purposes. (Note: the rule is different for estate tax purposes.)

As to a charitable donee, you can confirm its tax-exempt status by requesting proof of its 501(c)(3) filing status with the Internal Revenue Service. (This is the tax code section that applies to tax-exempt organizations.)

Any registered organization should be able to provide you with such proof, or you can check IRS Publication No. 78, which provides a cumulative list of exempt organizations.

Who Pays the Gift Tax?

What if you wanted to make a gift of more than the $10,000 maximum and it's not to a spouse or charitable organization, or for some exempt purpose? What happens then?

Then you fill out a gift tax return, and report the transfer to the IRS. I know this is a scary thought, but you do it for income taxes every year, and the good news is that it doesn't necessarily mean you owe any taxes.

How can this be? The answer lies in the Unified Gift and Estate Tax Credit ("Unified Credit" for short).

I capitalize Unified Credit to emphasize its importance to most people. It's unified because it applies to both gift and estate taxes as one credit, which makes some sense when you stop to think about it. A gift is a transfer before death; an estate transfer, whether done by Will or by trust, is a transfer after death. It's simply a difference in timing. What Congress has done in the tax code is to combine these taxes, giving a credit of $192,800.

"Wait a minute," you say. "I heard it was $600,000. What is this $192,800?"

It's the same thing, just put into different terms. The $192,800 is the *credit* against *taxes* owed, which equates to protecting a *gross* taxable estate of exactly $600,000.

For simplicity's sake, because it's easier to look at things based on the size of the estate rather than the amount of taxes—which involves going into the rate tables and doing multiplication—most people refer to this as the $600,000 exemption.

As you might imagine, this exemption covers a lot of estates, making them nontaxable as far as federal estate taxes are concerned. But before it starts protecting your taxable estate, it's hard at work protecting you from lifetime gift taxes—which would hurt even more, since you'd otherwise have to pay these while you're still alive.

What this means to you is that during your lifetime you can give away (if you're so generous) up to $600,000 in money or property gift tax free, over and above the $10,000 annual exclusion. Put another way, you do not pay any gift tax until your taxable gifts exceed this $600,000 mark for nonexempt, nonexcluded gifts.

Using this credit during your lifetime to avoid gift tax will reduce the amount of credit available to your estate after death, but that's then and this is now. If you have a mind to give, it's certainly better if you don't have to pay taxes while you're still alive.

But let's say there is a gift tax owing, to get to the final point of this section. Being the philanthropist that you are, you make lifetime nonexempt gifts of over $600,000, and now you want to give more. (You obviously believe in the saying "Give till it hurts.") Who pays the tax?

Well, primarily you do. The person who makes the gift, the donor, is primarily liable to pay the taxes. However, as a warning to you donees (gift recipients) out there, if the donor doesn't pay, you have to.

What Kind of Transfers Are Not Considered Gifts?

Anything that is transferred for good and valuable consideration, at or near fair market value, is not a gift by definition. There are, in addition, situations when it may appear that a gift is being made, but in fact it's not. For example:

I want to create a revocable living trust, but I'm concerned about gift taxes to my beneficiaries. Am I making a taxable gift today to people who may get my property after I die?

The operative word here is *may*. Because the beneficiaries may not ever get the property, there is no completed gift and therefore no taxable gift. If a beneficiary eventually does get property through this trust (after the settlor dies), then the gift has been made, but it's a gift after death and so covered by the estate tax.

Another example of this occurs in joint bank accounts when a person deposits money under his name and the name of another jointly. This may be, and typically is, done as a substitute for a Will. The person who puts the money into the account does not intend to part with ownership immediately, only to make arrangements so that the money can be obtained easily by the joint owner if he dies. In such a case, the gift is considered incomplete until the money is withdrawn.

Note, however, that this is not true when real property owned by one person is put into a joint tenancy with another. As discussed in the chapter on joint tenancy, this *is* considered a completed gift on transfer because the new joint owner can use or do with the property as he or she wishes immediately. A very thin distinction, I admit, but a reality of the law.

How Is the Gift Tax Determined?

If you're in the happy position to have given away enough money or property to merit a gift tax, the tax is charged against you based on the Uniform Gift and Estate Tax rate tables. In other words, like an income tax. You determine the amount of the gift that exceeds your lifetime exemption of $600,000, and you pay taxes based on the excess. Note, however, that gifts are accumulated over time, and as they increase above this limit (without other exclusions or exemptions), there is an increasing marginal rate that plateaus at 55 percent. A marginal gift and estate tax rate table is included for your review in the chart on page 188.

Even if you do not reach the $600,000 limit during your lifetime, the nonexempt gifts you make will accumulate year after year and be assessed against your allowable $600,000 for estate tax purposes.

Gift and Estate Tax Rates (Unified Rate Schedule) 1994

Amounts subject to tax:

Exceeding:	But not exceeding:	Tax	Tax rate on excess amount
$	$ 10,000	$ 0	18
10,000	20,000	1,800	20
20,000	40,000	3,800	22
40,000	60,000	8,200	24
60,000	80,000	13,000	26
80,000	100,000	18,200	28
100,000	150,000	23,800	30
150,000	250,000	38,800	32
250,000	500,000	70,800	34
500,000	750,000	155,800	37
750,000	1,000,000	248,300	39
1,000,000	1,250,000	345,800	41
1,250,000	1,500,000	448,300	43
1,500,000	2,000,000	555,800	45
2,000,000	2,500,000	780,800	49
2,500,000	3,000,000	1,025,800	53
3,000,000	10,000,000	1,290,800	55
10,000,000	21,040,000	5,140,800	60
21,040,000	—	11,764,800	65

As an example, if you had a net taxable estate of $950,000, you would calculate the tax as follows:

1. locate where $950,000 falls on the chart (this is between $750,000 and $1,000,000);

2. note that the tax for this range is $248,300 plus 39 percent of the excess;

3. calculate the tax by multiplying $200,000 (the excess) by .39, which equals $78,000; and

4. add this to $248,000 to determine the estate tax due, which is $326,000.

5. From this amount you can subtract your unified credit of $196,200, and any other credits you may be entitled to.

What Is an Estate Tax?

The estate tax is a tax paid by your estate for giving away your property after you die. As we have seen, it's tied closely to the gift tax by uniform tax rate tables and credits. It also allows the same deductions and contains many of the same rules as the gift tax. Thus, like the gift tax, there is an unlimited marital deduction for property that goes to your spouse. This means you can transfer as much as you want to your spouse, estate tax free. Note, however, that this is not true if your spouse is not a U.S. citizen. In such a case, there's no deduction unless the property is put into a qualified domestic trust in which at least one trustee is a U.S. citizen and the spouse gets only an income interest. (Note that there's no $100,000 exclusion here as there is from gift taxes annually for a noncitizen spouse.)

There is also an estate tax charitable deduction for gifts made after death to tax-exempt organizations, just as there is with gifts made during your lifetime.

The estate tax is determined by the size of the net estate. Generally, to assess your potential estate tax liability you start by taking the total value of all your assets and then deducting your debts. This is approximately your net estate for estate tax purposes. If this net estate is less than $600,000 and you haven't worked down your exemption with taxable gifts, you would not be subject to estate taxes, at least not if you die right away. Of course, if you live and the value of your estate increases for whatever reason, as it will often do, you may find that your estate later exceeds this $600,000 exemption.

Take heart—if your estate exceeds this amount, you can still use the marital or charitable deduction to reduce its size below this tax barrier. Remember, however, that giving after death, like giving during life, only makes sense when it's what you want to do. You cannot justify giving away a large chunk of money exclusively for tax reasons since the taxes saved will always be just a portion (based on the tax rate) of the total value lost by making the gift.

Who Pays the Estate Tax?

Note that the estate tax, unlike an inheritance tax that applies in some states, is assessed (charged) against the estate of the decedent, not the beneficiary. This point often seems misunderstood as the next frequently asked question shows:

My father just died leaving me his house, car, and a machine shop worth over $1 million. I am named in his Will as executrix as well as sole heir. The problem is the tax. The house and machine shop are not really salable in this market, and he left no cash. Am I personally liable for the taxes?

No. The estate, or more particularly, the assets of the estate are liable. The person who inherits will only inherit the debts of the estate, including the taxes, if they are willing to accept them. And in my experience, most people are willing to accept debts only if they receive something (the assets) of greater value in return. In this case, therefore, the caller need not accept the gift, or for that matter, she need not even accept the position as executrix, and if she doesn't she will have no personal obligation to pay the taxes or other debts of the estate.

On the other hand, why not accept the liability in this case? If the property really has a fair market value of over one million dollars, it should be salable for that amount, and since the taxes are always a percentage (no more than 55 percent) of the net taxable estate (gross value, less debts, over $600,000), there should be a net positive value here (a *large* net positive value).

If the property, however, is really not salable for this price, she should check the valuation, because by definition the fair market value is the price at which a reasonable buyer will buy and a reasonable seller will sell, neither being under any compulsion to do so. Thus, if a reasonable buyer cannot be found at this price, it cannot reflect the true fair market value. A lower fair market value would mean less taxes.

In either case, the point here is that the estate pays the estate tax out of the estate assets. If there are no assets, there are no taxes. If there are taxes, then there must be assets of greater value than the debts and expenses to cover them.

The best thing a person planning an estate can do to avoid this problem is to create a pool of funds (from, say, life insurance) to pay these taxes so that the estate assets need not be sold to cover this liability. The next best thing is to specify which assets will be sold to pay any liabilities or estate taxes owed. If this is not done, the IRS rules provide that estate taxes are to be taken out of all property pro rata (equally, based on value). This means that all property in your estate will have to bear the burden of its share of the estate tax, and may thus have to be sold to meet this obligation. If this is the result you want, fine, otherwise use your power to specify.

Several states have passed something called an "inheritance tax," which can be distinguished from the federal estate tax in that it's assessed against the beneficiaries or receivers of a gift rather than the estate itself. These states include Connecticut, Delaware, Indiana, Iowa, Kansas, Kentucky, Louisiana, Michigan, Oklahoma, Pennsylvania, South Dakota, and Tennessee. Note that these inheritance taxes often exempt certain people and provide different rate tables for different classes of persons. Even with regard to such taxes, however, the obligation only applies if the recipient agrees to accept the gift. Remember, you can always refuse or *disclaim* the inheritance. It's your choice.

When Do You File an Estate Tax Return and How Do You Calculate the Tax?

This is easy. You file nine months after death (unless you get an extension) if the gross value of the estate is greater than $600,000. Notice that the determination to file is based on the *gross* value of the estate—or the total assets *without* reduction for debts. Thus, an estate tax return must be filed even when no tax will be owed because the estate debts reduce the net estate below the $600,000 mark.

This brings up another question: Who must do the filing? There has to be someone who figures out what is owed, files the return, and pays the tax. The decedent is dead, so he's no good. So it has to be either the executor of the Will or the trustee of the trust, or if neither of these exists, the joint tenant of joint tenancy property. The responsibility falls on one of them to do whatever is necessary to determine the taxes and file the return.

The calculation involves four basic parts:

(1) determining the value of the assets and amount of the debts;
(2) netting these out and subtracting the deductions for marital and charitable gifts, and the administrative expenses of processing the estate;
(3) determining the tax by applying the result of this calculation, less Unified Credit, to the Unified Rate Schedule (see page 188); and
(4) subtracting any state tax credits allowable.

How Do You Value Property for Estate Tax Purposes?

About the trickiest part of calculating estate taxes, and the only part the executor or trustee has much control over, is the valuation of the estate assets. The court doesn't do it, and the IRS doesn't do it (at least on first blush). The executor does it, subject to the redetermination or challenge by the court, the beneficiaries, and the IRS.

Valuation can be either a complicated affair or extremely simple, based on the type of property. For example, stocks traded on major exchanges are easy to value. All you need to do is look at the stock price on the date of death.

Real estate, on the other hand, is not so easy. An executor can go to the newspaper, the neighbors, a real estate broker, a real estate appraiser, or anything in between, to get or justify his or her guesstimate as to the fair market value of a piece of property, but in general, a good real estate valuation requires the use of an expert, independent appraiser.

At one extreme, a clear way to determine value is to put the property up for sale and see what it brings. Since valuation can be made at the time of death or at an alternative valuation date six months following death, if you sell the property during this time (barring fluctuations in the market), the sale price can be used as its value.

No matter which method you use—short of selling the property—valuation is often little more than intelligent guesswork. The executor or his appraiser compare, as best they can, the property being valued to others of like size and quality that have sold in the area, and then make a determination of value. Even when it's a kind of property bought and sold regularly in public, there can be some guesswork as to the exact value based on the particular time at which the item is to be valued.

One interesting phenomenon I've observed concerning valuation of property in a probate/estate tax setting is that while it's the same procedure as valuation of property in other settings (getting a home loan, for example), the goal is often just the opposite. In a typical valuation, the owner seeks to obtain the highest possible valuation for his property. In a probate or estate tax situation, he seeks to obtain the lowest possible valuation in order to reduce taxes and probate fees.

Unfortunately, many people forget this and actually try to obtain a higher valuation than necessary. This, of course, can lead to higher taxes or a higher cost of probate. Thus, when valuing property for estate purposes, work toward the "fire sale" value of the property—what could you get for it if you had to sell by tomorrow.

How Do the Deductions for Marital and Charitable Bequests and Administrative Expenses Apply to Estate Taxes?

Marital and charitable bequests, as in the case of a lifetime gift, are deductible without limit from the gross estate. Thus, someone who gives away all (or everything except $600,000 worth) of their assets to charity or to their spouse after death, will pay no estate taxes. This is assuming, as we have discussed, the spouse is a U.S. citizen, the charity is certified as tax-exempt, and there were no excessive nonexempt lifetime gifts made.

What Are the Tax-Saving Tricks That Go into an Estate Plan?

"Enough of this blathering on about calculations and gift giving," you say. "I'm not much of a giver, and certainly not over $10,000 a year [it's hard for most people to imagine someone they like that much], and I'll be too dead to calculate anything at the time my estate is probated. Let's get to the good stuff—tax avoidance! How do I save estate taxes?"

There are several tricks, but I should warn you up front, they're really not worth much. Estate tax planning is far more limited than most people believe; possibly due to the fact that most estates are under $600,000, or will go to a spouse or charity and not be taxed at all.

Be that as it may, here are a few key estate tax planning devises most often asked about:

1. *Giving Away Property During Your Lifetime.*

This "trick" was discussed at the beginning of this chapter, so we need only make the connection to the obvious estate tax benefit. If you can give away less than $10,000 worth of property per year to each donee, you can reduce your estate by that amount, without any corresponding reduction in your unified credit. This is particularly effective with a gift of life insurance, as long as it's made more than three years before death—as was noted earlier.

But don't run out and start giving away your property yet (as if you were going to). Besides the obvious problem of not owning it anymore, there can be a hidden tax disadvantage. Consider the following scenario:

> **I have three children, all adults, who I would like to give my house. The house is worth about $250,000, and is pretty much all I own outright. I bought it in 1962 for $27,000 and paid off the mortgage, so there is no debt on the property. I should also point out that I trust my kids, without question, not to take advantage of the situation. If I ever wanted the house back they would certainly do so. Will I avoid probate and estate taxes by doing this?**

First, as you already know, if this is all this caller has of value, there are no estate taxes to avoid. Second, if he wants to avoid probate, he could set up a trust, or if this is too complicated, put the property into joint tenancy, rather than transfer it outright.

What does it matter if he really can trust the kids? The answer comes from the earlier discussion regarding basis.

He bought this property in 1962 for $27,000. Thus, assuming he made no capital improvements, his basis in the house is $27,000 (basis = cost + capital improvements). If he gives it to the kids before he dies and they sell it for the $250,000 he says it's worth, they will have to pay income taxes on the gain ($250,000 − $27,000 = $223,000). This is because their basis would be his basis.

If, however, they inherit the property rather than get it as a gift during his life, they get a step-up in basis to the value of the property on the date of his death. This means their basis upon his death would be $250,000, leaving a net taxable gain of zero if they sell it immediately ($250,000 − $250,000).

So, I repeat, why would this guy want to give his house away to his kids, doing them the disservice of increasing their tax burden at its sale? You will find this to be a potential tax disadvantage in all situations in which a person is trying to give away appreciated property before death.

Inheriting property for this purpose includes most situations in which the property passes to a beneficiary as part of the decedent's taxable estate. Consequently, taking property by Will, trust, or even joint tenancy (when the decedent puts up all the cost of the property) qualifies for this treatment.

2. Setting Up a Marital Life Trust (A-B Trust).

Now we're getting into the stuff that locker room whispers are made of. The secrets of the wealthy in avoiding estate taxes (and since you have to be a little wealthy to have an estate tax concern, this would be the interested group): a marital life trust—it sounds so important.

In reality, however, it's not all that complicated or difficult to set up. Indeed, there are several self-help books and computer programs that offer standardized forms for such a trust, costing between twenty and sixty dollars.

The basic premise behind a marital life trust is taking maximum advantage of the $600,000 exemption when a married couple is involved. Here's the situation:

You have a net taxable estate of $1 million, a wife (or husband), and two adult children. Like most people, when you die (if you die first) you want your estate to go to your spouse, and then, when he or she dies, to your kids. If you die first, because of the unlimited spousal deduction, there are no estate taxes at all. This is good.

But look at what has happened. By transferring all your assets to your spouse, your spouse now has a $1 million estate all lumped together. When he or she dies and transfers the property to the kids, there will be an estate tax on the excess $400,000 transferred. This is not good.

By doing things this way, you have, in effect, wasted the $600,000 exemption of the first spouse to die. It all went to a spouse and so was deducted anyway. A marital life trust, on the other hand, would take advantage of this otherwise wasted exemption.

To understand how it works, start with a regular living trust created by a husband and wife jointly, as joint trustees. A marital life estate starts like this, but then after one of the spouses dies, his or her share gets divided out into an irrevocable subtrust—often called the "B trust." The living spouse's half, the "A trust," remains revocable and under his or her complete control.

The B trust is divided between the surviving spouse and the kids. The spouse gets a life interest in the property and the kids get the remainder. A life interest is generally the right to the interest, use, or profits of the property during the person's life, subject to the right of the remainder person to the principal or corpus after the life interest holder dies.

What does this division do? Among other things, it

takes one half of the trust property out of the surviving spouse's estate. Thus, when he or she dies, the property passes to the children without estate taxes (or probate fees).

Let's use the above example to see how all this works. If the husband had died leaving $400,000 of his half of the trust property to the kids in the B trust, and the remaining $100,000 to his wife outright or in the A trust (instead of all to his wife), there would be no estate taxes owed because of the $600,000 exemption. Moreover, now the wife has only a $600,000 estate for tax purposes (within the credit amount), so when she dies no taxes will be owed (assuming the estate doesn't grow further after his death). The trick here is that she has only a "life" interest in the $400,000 B trust, and so it doesn't get included in her estate when she dies. Isn't it nice how things work out just right when you plan carefully?

Consequently, this type of trust won't be of any value if your estate is under $600,000, and will have proportionately diminishing worth as your estate rises above $1.2 million. It's also of no value if you're not married or don't care who gets your property after both you and your spouse die.

Besides these limitations, there are a few other problems with using a marital life trust. (By the way, you can now see where this instrument gets its name—it's a marital trust in which a life estate is created.) Consider this situation:

Before he died, my husband and I created a marital life trust. He was sixty-two and I'm now fifty-eight. My problem is that while our kids are doing

just fine, I need to get to some of the money in the trust that is set aside for a big income tax debt he left. How can I do this?

The obvious problem is that she's no longer the sole owner of all the property. The property in the life estate is hers for life only, which means the kids have a remainder interest that she cannot waste, spend, or disturb in any way. If she was in her seventies or eighties this might not be such a big deal, but a woman in her fifties can have a lot of life ahead, and that's a long time to have property tied up in order to avoid estate taxes.

Another disadvantage, although this questioner may not have realized it yet (her husband had only recently died), is that she will have to maintain separate books and records and file a tax return for the B trust. The same thing that created the tax savings, the separate irrevocable subtrust, creates the limitation on access and the hassle of separate record keeping. As we say in the law, there's always a quid pro quo (literally, something for something).

Having said all this, there are still things that can be done for someone in this situation depending on the circumstances. First, if she can get all the kids (beneficiaries) to agree, they should be able to revoke the trust and distribute the property to her. This, of course, would be a gift from the kids to the mother of their remainder interests. Such interest would thus have to be valued and could affect the children's unified credit amount if the gift was large enough. In addition, this action would, at the very least, undo whatever estate tax benefits the marital life estate trust was designed to create.

Another option is to work within the trust itself. The

tax laws allow such trusts to be set up so that the trustee (usually the surviving spouse) can invade the corpus (take the principal for her own purposes) in an emergency situation for health or other basic necessities of life. For this to work, the need of the surviving spouse must not only qualify as an emergency as described in the trust document, this ability to invade corpus must have been part of the trust terms before the husband died. It cannot be added after the fact.

Under the tax laws, the trustee can also be given what's known as a 5 and 5 power—the unrestricted right to distribute to the survivor (again only if it's in the trust document before the death) up to a maximum of 5 percent of the trust, or $5,000, whichever is greater.

On the other hand, the trust may be more restrictive, placing limits on a surviving spouse's access to even the interest income of the trust. It's all a matter of how the trust was set up, and there's obviously a lot of flexibility in this regard.

One last thing on this little trust trick. If more than $600,000 goes into the B portion of the trust (to the kids), the excess is taxable and the tax must be paid at the time the first spouse dies. One way to avoid this is through a Q-TIP (Qualified Terminal Interest Property) trust. A Q-TIP trust is a marital life trust in which there's no tax on the amount above $600,000 until after the life owner dies. Note, however, that it's all taxed at that time. Since Q-TIPs are not frequently asked about, I do not discuss them here in much detail.

3. Setting Up a Generation-Skipping Trust.

A generation-skipping trust is just what it sounds like—a trust designed to skip a generation in terms of estate taxes. It works something like a marital life trust, dividing the right and interest in trust property between a life owner and a remainder person or persons. With a generation-skipping trust, however, the life estate is owned by the children, and the remainder is held by the grandchildren.

The result is that the children have limited access to the trust property, and consequently it's not taxed as part of their estate when they die. The *negative* is that the property is locked up as far as the children are concerned, and there is an estate tax on the initial transfer when the parent(s) die if the amount is over $600,000—and if it's not, then why bother? The *positive* is that there is no estate tax on the property when the children die. The old quid pro quo.

For the extremely wealthy, this might be a neat trick to avoid estate taxes while keeping property in the family for multiple generations; however, the government has other plans. It likes to collect its tax upon each transfer to each younger generation, so it's developed rules to limit this maneuver. Basically, these rules say you can only have $1 million protected in such a trust (enough for most people, but remember this is a trust most often used by the very wealthy) before the estate tax will be applied to the children's estate regardless of their limited life interest. This is all done by imposition of a generation-skipping transfer tax.

4. *Setting Up an Irrevocable Trust for Property That Will Likely Appreciate.*

We have already discussed the downside to irrevocable trusts in Chapter 4—they're irrevocable and later you may need or want access to the trust corpus. If you're willing to take this risk, however, one way to get tax benefits is to give away property that's likely to appreciate in value. The idea is to give the property away when it has relatively low value, making the gift tax effects small, and then, when you die and it's worth more, it's out of your estate and not subject to the estate tax. This, in effect, minimizes the negative impact on the unified credit.

Of course, you may need a crystal ball to choose property that is likely to appreciate, and you must be willing to irreversibly part with ownership and control in order to get the estate tax benefits.

5. *Disclaiming Property: After-the-Fact Tax Saving.*

One of my favorite estate planning questions of all time is not really a planning question, but a cleanup question made necessary from a lack of planning. Here's how it goes:

> **My father just died leaving everything to my mother—an estate of about $1.1 million dollars. I've done some checking and I understand there's no estate taxes due on this amount because it's all covered by the marital deduction. What I'm concerned about are the taxes due after she dies. She**

**is currently seventy-two and my sister and I will
need to take care of her financial affairs anyway.
How can we avoid estate taxes then?**

As you may have recognized, this is a classic set of
circumstances calling for a marital life trust. The problem
is that it's too late to do this. The father is dead.

So what can be done, if anything?

The answer is to have the mother disclaim all or part
of the inheritance. To disclaim means to refuse to accept.
By disclaiming, the property goes automatically to the residuary beneficiary under the Will, or if there is no Will or
the disclaimer is done by the residuary beneficiary, then
to the next of kin. Nicely enough, in this case, the disclaimed property would go to the two daughters.

In effect, this keeps the property out of the mother's
estate and passes it to the children, without incurring gift
or estate tax—as long as the amount of property transferred is less than $600,000.

In order to disclaim under current tax laws, the disclaimer must be irrevocable and unconditional and meet
all of the following criteria:

(1) It must be in writing, describe the interest
    disclaimed, and be signed by the disclaimant.
(2) It must be received by the transferor, his legal
    representative, or, if he is dead, the executor or
    administrator of his estate, within nine months
    of the transfer. The date of the transfer for gift
    tax purposes is when the gift is made. The date
    of the transfer for estate tax purposes is the
    date of death.

(3) The disclaimant must not have accepted the interest or any of the benefits of the interest in the property.

In addition, the person making the disclaimer cannot exercise any control over the property disclaimed. This means he or she cannot designate who gets the property following the disclaimer. The property must pass naturally to the next person in line by Will or law.

Under the facts given above, this works out just fine and it makes sense, if she wants to do this, for the mother to disclaim enough property given her to reduce her estate down to her allowable credit—$600,000, unless she's used some of it up in lifetime gifts.

What Is the Effect of State Inheritance and Estate Taxes on an Estate Plan?

The answer is "not much." Less than half the states even have death-based taxes (these include Connecticut, Delaware, Indiana, Iowa, Kansas, Kentucky, Louisiana, Massachusetts, Michigan, Mississippi, New York, Ohio, Oklahoma, Pennsylvania, Rhode Island, South Dakota, and Tennessee), and many of these are of the "pickup tax" variety—meaning they are set to exactly equal the federal credit so that there is no *net* tax effect.

Among the states that do have these taxes, there are generally two kinds: estate taxes and inheritance taxes. The main difference is that with an estate tax the tax is against the estate, while with an inheritance tax the tax is against the person who inherits.

States that have such taxes will generally try to apply them to persons who are domiciled in (are residents of) their state at the time of their death. These taxes can also be applied to death transfers of real estate located in the state.

Most people will not move to another state or establish residency just to avoid estate taxes. The cost is generally greater than the potential benefits. However, if you're one of the few who can obtain a net benefit by such a move, you should know that residency for this purpose is a matter of the facts and circumstances of your living situation, including things like where you vote, get your mail, live most of the time, and work.

CHAPTER TEN

Probate Procedure

I remember several years back being called by a friend and asked to go with him to visit his sick mother. It was an "official" visit, he told me; she was dying and she wanted to take care of her affairs. I agreed, although I generally dread such visits, for obvious reasons.

When I met with her in her bedroom, however, I was surprised by how healthy she looked, so I inquired about her illness.

"What is it you have?" I asked.

"I can't say," she replied.

"Well, what does your doctor say?"

"Oh, I haven't seen any doctor."

"Then how do you know you're dying?"

"I just know, and I'm only holding on until you do what needs to be done."

"Are you really certain? Because it makes a difference. If you know you're going to die, and you're sure, then there's one way to handle your affairs. If you're not absolutely positive, then there's another."

"I'm as sure as I was born," she said. "And don't feel bad, because I'm comfortable with the thought of it, and not scared. I just want to make sure my things are taken care of."

Her estate was small, certainly under the $600,000 exemption, but it contained several items that were recorded, like a house, some stock, and a car. We made a list of her assets, and then went about the process of transferring them outright to the names of her children and other beneficiaries, as she requested. As I saw it, there were only two objectives to this estate plan: make sure each piece of property got into the hands of the family member she'd intended, and avoid probate. In view of the size of the estate, we had no tax concerns.

Looking back, I have to admit that I was a little nervous about this outright transfer plan. She had originally asked me only for a Will—she had no knowledge of what else she could do—and I had mentioned that she could just make the transfers she wanted to as outright gifts to avoid probate. I thought that despite her apparent certainty of imminent death, she would reject such an extreme plan.

On the contrary, however, she embraced it, insisting that we do just that, "as long as it's legal," she said. I assured her it was legal, but reminded her of the consequences if she lived.

"Suppose by some happy circumstance you live, as we all hope you do. If you give all your property away, you won't have it anymore."

To which she replied, "Thank you for the thought, but I'm certain."

I made several other suggestions, including a trust, but they were all rejected except for a backup Will I absolutely insisted upon. In the face of such certainty I agreed to help her make the outright transfers, but only after she had signed off on a letter I had prepared explaining her options (a standard method of C.Y.A., covering your ass, for attorneys).

She did so, and not twenty-four hours after I informed her everything was done, she was dead. I'll never forget the eerie chill that came over me when my friend called to give me the news.

"How did she die?" I asked.

"In her sleep," he said. "Her heart just gave out."

"How did she know it was going to happen?"

I thought I heard a crack in his voice as he said, "Mama always just knew."

A few months later I got another call from him, and in the midst of the conversation he asked what he should do about his mother's car.

"Wasn't that given to your sister?" As I recalled, it had been.

"Not that car," he said. "The Cadillac."

"What are you talking about? She had only one car, the Buick."

"Not so." He pointed out, "There's an old classic Cadillac by the side of her house. It was jointly owned by her and my father before he died. It's not in great shape, and hasn't been driven much, but I think it's worth a few thousand cleaned up."

Instead of a chill, this time a flush came over me. An old Cadillac, probably still in the old man's name along with his wife's—it meant one thing, the thing we had so actively tried to avoid: probate.

"How come no one ever told me about this before?"

I think I must have sounded a little angry, or at least a little defensive.

"Probably never thought about it," he replied, apparently oblivious to what this all meant. "It's not really that big a deal."

I told him what it meant from the legal standpoint, and he seemed less concerned than I was. After all, to him it was just a procedure, and the family had gotten the bulk of the assets outside of probate, without the delay or cost, so this seemed like small potatoes.

Even so, it was an irritation, a pain in the behind to have to prepare and file the paperwork for one relatively small item. We found out it was worth about $3,500, so it couldn't be trashed. The backup Will took effect (it went to all the kids equally), and about four months later we were able to transfer title and sell the car.

One of the several morals I took from this experience is that there's never a guarantee you'll be able to completely avoid probate. You can use all the foresight in the world, plan as we did to give the property to others or transfer it into a trust, but there is always the possibility that something will be left out, and that something is usually something that will require probate.

And if you haven't planned, or the person who died and named you executor of his or her estate hadn't planned, there is an even greater likelihood of being trapped into this process.

It's therefore no surprise, despite all the great advice by all the experts on how to avoid probate, that many of the most frequently asked questions in the area of estate planning involve probate and its procedure.

What Is Probate?

To most people probate is something unknown and a little (or a lot) scary. It involves lawyers, accountants, courts, and paperwork, which means expense and time delays.

Probate is the legal process used to close off a person's legal and financial affairs after his or her death. In a nutshell, the process works like this: The executor identifies and values the assets and debts that are part of the estate, making sure the debts and administration expenses are paid and tax returns (income and estate) are filed, if necessary. Then he distributes the remaining assets to the beneficiaries and terminates the court process.

Simple? Not really. So, as you might expect, there are always a few questions along the way.

How Do You File a Probate Proceeding?

A growing number of people have recently been deciding to file and handle a probate procedure without the help of an attorney. As long as there is no complicated Will contest, which there most often is not, and as long as this is allowed by state law or probate court procedure, which it most often is not, this may be a reasonable task, especially for simple estates.

If you're determined not to hire an attorney either because of cost or personal beliefs, you might want to seek the help of an independent paralegal (IP). An independent paralegal, sometimes called a legal technician, is an unlicensed person who is often experienced at putting together legal paperwork and knowing where to file it. An IP is generally less expensive than an attorney, and can be of assistance in walking you through the process. You should note, however, that an IP cannot give legal advice or provide legal services beyond helping you fill out the forms and file them.

If you decide to use an IP, make sure he or she is familiar with the courts in your area and knows the proper forms to file for the area of law of concern—in this case probate.

The biggest problem with doing a probate yourself, as in many areas of law, is the filing procedures: the right forms, filed in the right place, at the right time.

The best situation, short of not being subject to probate, is to fall under a state exemption or simplified probate procedure law. These statutes are typically limited in amount and coverage, and come in two forms: summary procedures that allow for a simplified court process, and probate by affidavit.

What kind of summary procedures are allowed and under what conditions they can be used varies greatly from state to state, but they typically involve simplified form filings, often avoiding any court hearing, when the amount of the estate is below a set amount.

The second form of exemption, a probate by affidavit, allows for the transfer of property by simply filling out an affidavit and presenting it to the holder or registrar with evidence of your right (such as the Will and/or a death certificate). The good news is that such a procedure can amount to a complete avoidance of court delays and costs. The bad news is that this procedure is not often available, and when it is, it's very limited in the amount of property that can be transferred. States that have some form of affidavit procedure include Arizona, Arkansas, California, Colorado, Delaware, Hawaii, Idaho, Illinois, Indiana, Maine, Maryland, Montana, Nebraska, Nevada, New Mexico, New York, North Carolina, North Dakota, Oregon, South Carolina, South Dakota, Tennessee, Texas, Utah, Virginia, Washington, Wisconsin, and Wyoming.

Beyond summary procedures and exemptions lies the complicated mess of steps that so often constitute a probate process. While differences in state laws make it impossible for me to be specific on how it all works, on a general level a probate goes something as follows:

First, someone files a petition to probate the estate, announcing the basics: whether there is a Will or not; who is named the executor; whether that person has to post a bond; what assets are in the estate, and who are the beneficiaries. Many states provide standard forms for this, but that's not true everywhere.

Next, there's a notice that's filed with the court, mailed to beneficiaries of the Will, the next of kin, and any creditors, and typically published in a local paper for some period of time (usually three to four weeks).

A hearing is then held in which the executor or personal representative is appointed and his or her powers given. And that's when things start to move along. The executor identifies and gathers the estate assets, pays the debts, and finally distributes the remaining assets to the beneficiaries before closing off the estate.

How Do You Find the Assets and Debts of a Person Who Has Died?

This, maybe more than anything else, seems to scare the novice entering into the probate process. A lifetime collection of property and the debts that arise therefrom: where do you start to locate all this stuff?

Assuming you don't have a clue, which is rare, start by finding the decedent's private papers, checkbook, receipts, bills, and the like. Most often these are in his or her house somewhere or with an accountant or bookkeeper.

A person's bank records tell a lot more than just where he keeps his money. From this you can determine many of the person's debts and recent investments. For example, if you were to find a regular payment to a bank, you might suspect either a car or home loan.

In the decedent's paperwork you can also pick up things like promissory notes, stocks, bonds (or brokerage reports of stocks and bonds owned), copies of deeds, partnership agreements, insurance documents, copyrights, patents, and other things that show up mostly on paper. This can lead you to more tangible assets like real estate, cars, antiques, furniture, and personal items.

Identifying assets, however, doesn't necessarily mean you have them available for paying debts or making distributions, as this next example shows:

I have been appointed executor of my father's estate, which includes a partnership business he used to run with my brother. I think my brother resents the fact that my father made me the executor of his Will and not him, and so he's being difficult about giving me information about the business. What can I do to make him cooperate?

This type of question comes up in various forms, but always comes down to this: Once I've found an asset, how can I gain control over it?

The answer is to start by asking nicely, escalate into a demand letter, and then, if forced—and only if forced—get an order from the probate court requiring cooperation or the return of the property into the estate's control.

Like any court action, if this type of action can be avoided, you're better off. The cost in time, energy, and money to get the job done is always better avoided, especially when, as in this case, a family member is involved.

How Do You Find Beneficiaries?

You would think that most of the time the beneficiaries would find you. The image of salivating relatives, hovering like vultures around the poor decedent's estate, is something that's become almost a cliché in our society. Still, there are quite a few occasions, I have found, when the named beneficiary, or more often the next of kin, cannot be found or identified. This happens because the person has moved (maybe out of the country) and left no forwarding address, or because in the case of a next of kin, the person cannot be identified from family records. Here's an example:

> **I've been appointed the executrix of my aunt's estate, which includes a large gift to myself and all my cousins. I've been able to find all of them but three. I've checked around and no one seems to know where they went. Can I distribute their share to the others I have found, and if not, what do I do with their share?**

The other side to this is:

> **I think I was to receive an inheritance from my great-grandfather who lived back east before he died. How would I find out whether something is due me?**

The probate process is full of rules that set forth how things must be done, but in this area there's nothing set in stone except that if the rightful heir cannot be found, the executrix *cannot* just give the property to someone else.

If the rightful heir cannot be found, the property is typically held either in the estate or eventually by a state agency until he or she can be located. This means that the best place for an heir to start looking for his inheritance is in the probate court for the county where the decedent lived just prior to death. Check the records of the probate proceeding; it should provide information regarding the whereabouts of the money or property. Then follow that trail to either the executor of the estate or the state agency that holds unclaimed inheritances.

For a quick fix, if you're not sure of the state or location where the person died, but have a feeling your inheritance is out there, you can call the Lost Funds line, a 900 service that provides information on unclaimed inheritances as well as other funds held by state and federal agencies for persons who cannot be located. You can call our toll-free 800 line, 1-800-835-3529 to get the 900 number for this service. Note that there will be a cost for the 900 call, and you have to be eighteen years of age or older to use the service.

For the occasional executor who cannot locate an heir, be careful. You cannot just change the beneficiary because someone cannot be found. Their money is their money, and if someday they show up and you've given it away, say to all the other cousins as in the example above, you may find yourself personally liable for the entire amount.

A more prudent approach is to do a thorough investigation into the whereabouts of the person, and if he or she is found to be dead, then you can distribute the proceeds to the next in line or the person identified to take in the Will should the gift fail. If the person is just not found, procedures are usually set by the court to transfer that person's share to the state agency that holds such properties.

When Will They Distribute the Money, or How Long Does a Probate Take?

If there was ever one most commonly asked probate procedure–type question, this is it. When am I going to get the money? How can I get the attorney to speed up the process? Do you think the executor (if it's an attorney) is stalling the process to increase fees? It's all about time and money. Here is a typical question:

> **My father died five years ago and my brother has been in charge of probating the estate. He tells me little about what is going on, except that the attorney has not gotten the paperwork completed and that there are complications. Is this a normal length of time, and what can I do to get them to move it along?**

A typical probate will take about four months to a year, depending on the state it's in and what's involved. Can it be done in a shorter or longer time? Absolutely. Simplified probate procedures, which have been adopted in some states, can jet you through the process in less than thirty days, if they apply. On the other hand, I've heard of probates that have remained open for fifteen years or more.

What can make a probate last so long? Long delays usually involve a combination of lack of interest, or pure laziness, on the part of the people running the estate, and some complication with selling or otherwise handling an asset or finding or identifying a beneficiary.

Do attorneys stretch out the process to make higher fees? Sometimes. But, honestly, this is a rarity. Fees in many states are determined as a percentage of the estate, and they may even be fixed by law, which means attorneys have less incentive to do this sort of game playing. That is not to say such bad behavior is nonexistent, and you should note that even when fees are fixed by law there are often exemptions referred to as "extraordinary fees," which allow an attorney to charge extra when he or she does something special, like supervise the sale of estate property.

If you think the attorney or executor of an estate is stalling, because of fees, laziness, or otherwise, the best way to handle it is to call him or her and ask what's going on. Then, if this doesn't solve the problem, send a demand letter asking for a written explanation for the delay.

Along this line, it's important for a person who acts as the executor of an estate to keep the heirs informed of what's going on with the process, as the following situation shows:

I am named as an heir in my cousin's Will, which is being handled by another cousin of mine. I haven't heard a thing from her in three months,

but I understand she's moved into his house and is using some of his money to fix it up while she's living there. Can she do this, and what can I do to stop her?

She probably can, and you may not want to stop her. If the information this caller has is true, which it may or may not be, there could be several explanations. It could be, as the caller concluded, that the cousin has taken the house for her own use and benefit to the detriment of the other beneficiaries. Or, as it actually turned out, she could have been fixing it up to make the house salable for the benefit of all. It only took a direct inquiry to find this out, and avoid a dispute.

Lack of information, or misinformation, is by far the biggest cause of probate disputes—probate procedures that turn into court battles, which can be expensive and time consuming. When time goes by and the beneficiaries don't hear anything, or what they do hear they don't understand, or it conflicts with their expectations as to what should be happening, they get irritated, upset, challenging. The person acting as executor may then react negatively to the challenge as a sign of mistrust, which it may be, and the dispute escalates.

The better way is for the executor to provide, on a regular basis, full information to the beneficiaries on the nature and extent of the estate, assets, debts, and distributions. Most states require executors and trustees to do this upon demand in any case. If you are a beneficiary and want information about an estate, write to the executor asking for an accounting and any specific information you need. If you are an executor, keep the beneficiaries informed.

If you are having trouble getting answers to any of your questions regarding an ongoing probate, or for that matter any area of estate planning, feel free to call Tele-Lawyer and talk to an expert. We have the answers—and after buying this book, you have the opportunity to try out the service at no cost for the first five minutes. Give it a try.

GET UP TO FIVE MINUTES OF CONSULTATION FREE!

Simply send the completed coupon on the reverse side along with the original sales receipt for your purchase of this book to register to receive a free five-minute phone consultation with a lawyer from Tele-Lawyer, Inc.

In confidence, you can get advice on legal issues such as:

Bankruptcy • Divorce
Estate Planning • Taxes

For details about receiving the free five-minute phone call with Tele-Lawyer, please see the rules below. Be sure to save these rules until you make your call. Offer expires 2/1/96.

RULES FOR OBTAINING FREE FIVE-MINUTE TELE-LAWYER CALL

1. Offer expires on February 1, 1996. Call must have been completed by that date.

2. To receive the free five minutes, book purchasers must first send to Tele-Lawyer, Inc. at P.O. Box 110, Huntington Beach, CA 92648, their original store receipt for purchase of any FIVE-MINUTE LAWYER book together with the completed registration form provided. No copies or facsimiles of the coupon or store receipt will be accepted. Neither Tele-Lawyer nor the publisher is responsible for late, lost or misdelivered mail.

3. Following receipt of the registration form and sales slip, purchasers can call Tele-Lawyer between 8 a.m. to 6 p.m. PST, at 1-800-TELELAW (835-3529), and identify themselves by name and address. After the operator confirms that Tele-Lawyer has received caller's completed registration form and sales receipt, caller will be given a personal identification number and will be put through to an attorney who will attempt to answer caller's question. A credit card must be given at the start of the call to cover any excess attorney time beyond the free five minutes, unless the caller agrees to terminate the call immediately upon the expiration of the five minute period. The time begins at the moment the attorney connects with the client and ends at the time they hang up. Alternatively, the caller can ask the operator about using a 900-number method to place the call without using a credit card. (rules continued on back)

TELE-LAWYER FIVE-MINUTE LAWYER REGISTRATION FORM

Please complete, clip and return this form with your original sales receipt showing the purchase of a FIVE-MINUTE LAWYER book to: Tele-Lawyer, Inc., Five-Minute Free Call, P.O. Box 110, Huntington Beach, CA 92648.

(Please type or print)

Name: _____

Address: _____

City/State/Zip: _____

Phone: _____

Title of book and date purchased: _____

(rules continued)

4. Any call lasting longer than the alloted five minutes will be charged at the regular Tele-Lawyer rates (no other discounts will apply). Additional time charges will appear on the caller's phone bill or as a credit card charge. While Tele-Lawyer will make a good faith effort to service callers immediately, Tele-Lawyer does not guarantee the immediate availability of any of its attorneys. High volume and limited availability of specialists can result in delays of up to 24 hours, or longer.

5. Attorneys will attempt in good faith to answer all caller questions. There is no guarantee, however, that an attorney will be able to answer a caller's question in five minutes or less or otherwise help the caller in any way. Callers should be aware that some legal questions may not be answerable at all, and that there is no provision for refund of any additional free time. Tele-Lawyer is not responsible for any misunderstanding or misapplications by callers of advice or information provided by its attorneys.

6. A 10% discount can be obtained for further Tele-Lawyer services following the first call by providing the buyer's personal identification number obtained by registering, and calling the 800-number if the caller uses a credit card for billing purposes.